Digital Archives

Management, use and access

Digital Archives

Management, use and access

Edited by
Milena Dobreva

facet
publishing

Published by Facet Publishing,
7 Ridgmount Street, London WC1E 7AE
www.facetpublishing.co.uk

Facet Publishing is wholly owned by CILIP: the Library and
Information Association.
The editor and authors of the individual chapters assert their moral
right to be identified as such in accordance with the terms of the
Copyright, Designs and Patents Act 1988.

British Library Cataloguing in Publication Data
A catalogue record for this book is available from the British Library.

ISBN 978-1-85604-934-4 (paperback)
ISBN 978-1-78330-114-0 (hardback)
ISBN 978-1-78330-240-6 (e-book)

First published 2018

Text printed on FSC accredited material.

Typeset from editors' files by Flagholme Publishing Services in 11/14pt
Palatino and OpenSans
Printed and made in Great Britain by CPI Group (UK) Ltd, Croydon, CR0 4YY.

To A, a true friend, who motivated me to explore the challenges of reskilling information professionals.

Contents

List of Figures and Tables

Figures

Tables

Abbreviations

ADS	The Archaeology Data Service
AHA	American Historical Association
ARMA	International formerly the Association of Records Managers and Administrators
BYOD	bring your own device
CEO	Chief Executive Officer
CERN	Conseil Européen pour la Recherche Nucléaire (the European Organization for Nuclear Research)
CTO	Chief Technology Officer
CUDOS	Communalism; universalism; disinterestedness; organised scepticism
DAF	Data Audit Framework
DMP	Data Management Plan
DPLA	Digital Public Library of America
FAIR	findable, accessible, interoperable and re-usable
GPS	Global positioning system
HEI	Higher Education Institutions
ICA	International Council on Archives
Jisc	formerly the Joint Information Systems Committee (JISC)
MOOC	massive open online courses
NASA	National Aeronautics and Space Administration
NSIDC	National Snow and Ice Data Center
OA	open access
OCLC	Center Online Computer Library Center, Inc., founded as Ohio College Library Center
PSI	Public sector information
R&D	Research & Development
SAA	Society of American Archivists
VPN	virtual private network

Foreword

On a cold, rainy day in June 2017, I went to hear Richard Ovenden, the Bodley's Librarian (the senior executive position of the Bodleian Libraries of Oxford University) speak at the National Library of Ireland in Dublin. In his talk, entitled 'Curating Culture: research libraries in a digital age', Ovenden spoke about recent efforts at the Oxford libraries to document (then) current events. In particular, he mentioned the campaigning of June 2016 that led to the UK voting to leave the European Union (EU) (in what was sometimes described as the Brexit referendum). In the run-up to the referendum, the Leave the EU campaign had a 'battle bus', the brainchild of the Leave campaign director Dominic Cummings. Plastered on the double decker was a large sign that said 'We send the EU £350 million a week. Let's fund our NHS [National Health Service] instead. Vote Leave.'

On 23 June 2016, after the referendum results were announced, the £350 million figure was declared wildly exaggerated (the Office for National Statistics noted that it did not take into account rebates and payments to the public sector from the EU). Furthermore, Nigel Farage, one of the key architects of the Brexit campaign, noted that any savings would not go to the NHS after all and implied that had never been promised. Even in April 2017, prominent pro-Brexit campaigner and politician Boris Johnson stood by that £350 million figure, but the bus vanished the day after the referendum.

Photos of the bus placard still exist on the web, though, however much its creators would want them to have vanished. The image is also contained within the curated web archives of the Bodleian Library of Oxford University, along with other ephemera and social media around the referendum. Ovenden noted that in spite of difficulties over re-use of digital information and legal deposit in the UK context, the process of web archiving strikes an important blow against those who would try to erase or minimise acts of recent history.

A snapshot of July 2017, a month later: the international news is dominated by concerns about the Trump family and staff's contacts and emails with Russian operatives before the US election of November 2016. Closer to home here in Europe, there is ongoing uncertainty about the effects Brexit will have on the political and economic landscape. Both of these situations were still in force in January 2018. My social media feeds at the time were full of comments from friends and colleagues who are non-British EU citizens working in the UK. These people are concerned about their status in the post-Brexit UK, where they anticipate they will live without full freedom of movement and work, something they have accepted will occur as they are citizens of other EU countries. Several colleagues who have lived in the UK for more than five years are frantically unearthing documents from their attics and filing cabinets to prove their residency for the purpose of obtaining permanent residency status (the British government requires 'paper' copies of bills and receipts as proof, even though many people use paperless billing. Banks and utilities must now provide – at a price – paper copies since printouts are not considered acceptable).

On an even more local and personal scale, during the summer of 2017, my husband was assembling his paperwork to become naturalised in Ireland. He initially applied in August 2016 with copies of his US passport and other relevant documents witnessed by a commissioner of oaths. However, the regulations for the required paperwork had changed in autumn 2017. He was asked to provide more documents to comport with regulations that were only introduced after he applied. He was frustrated, but he is a cautious person and had carefully labelled boxes of documents in the attic with copies of our leases, utility bills and bank statements going back to 2011 when we moved to Dublin. Furthermore, we have lived in the same house with the same utilities for the six years we have been in Ireland (and thank goodness the Irish government accepts digital copies of our paperless utility bills as proof of residence). As part of the process, he also obtained and submitted certified copies of his birth certificate from the small hamlet in West Virginia where he was born. The West Virginia records office and local archives was flooded not long after from unprecedented storms. After navigating the multiple bureaucracies involved, he received his citizenship in November 2017.

What these anecdotes share is that they illustrate some of the many important roles that archives (and records) play in our lives, individually and collectively, and the potential consequences of the medium in which such records are captured or created. We all participate in webs of activity that are increasingly recorded in paper, digital and hybrid forms. All records can be endangered or rendered unreadable by malicious activity, neglect, natural disaster or the ephemerality of their formats, with potentially grave consequences. How do individuals and archival institutions make choices about digitisation and the digital?

The goal of this book is to explore the latter: archives and archival practices in the digital realm. Richard Ovenden's talk reminded me that archives and archival practice form a bulwark against those consequences. Archives collectively tell us that things happen, things need to be remembered, and words and documents and images matter to all of us. Archives are honest brokers in our collective need to remember and document. Hundreds of images of the Brexit bus can be found with a quick search of Google, even as politicians and others with an agenda deny or at best minimise the importance or relevance of those images. These images can be altered with ease. However, when the Bodleian Libraries archive that image and give it its imprimatur – along with hundreds of other images, documents, stories and social media – the image, its context, meaning and importance come to the fore as an artefact of memory.

These anecdotes also illustrate another topic that is at the heart of this volume: the digital complicates the concept of the record and the archives. Digital access does not make access simpler. Instead, it raises questions in a number of directions. With the sheer quantity of material available for digitisation and the increasing amount of born digital information available, archives are making choices and justifying to their stakeholders what to make available in digital format. Users are keen to have digital access to materials in distant archives and special collections, but archivists have to make hard choices about what to digitise. Should they focus on the most 'popular' items, the 'rarest' items, the most fragile items, or should they be digitising on demand? There are also other worries. As digital collections increase in volume, the need for technical and human infrastructure also increases. Where will the resources to keep materials available come from, how can digital collections and the institutions that house them be sustained over time, and what business models will weather change? Will digitising reduce the demand for physical access to the archives or to particular parts of the collection? (Ovenden says no; many of the collections at Oxford's libraries have experienced increased demand, not less, in the wake of digitisation).

There are technical challenges with providing access that are complex in the digital realm. For example, most archivists and librarians have heard (and cringed at) the question: 'Why do you need to organise materials when we have full text and Google search available?' There are many answers to this (sometimes) innocently posed question but putting digital and digitised materials online without organisation is a recipe for chaos. Ensuring preservation and authenticity over time in an era where physical custody is not always possible entails a host of organisational and technical challenges. Well-constructed metadata, a robust digital preservation strategy, collection development strategy and appraisal are necessary to make digital materials trustworthy and accessible over time.

Archives are also responding to the changing nature of user expectations and needs and the evolution of disciplines that are themselves working through the implications of digital access to archival objects. Research disciplines are not only users of digital information but creators in the form of texts, data in myriad formats (simple and complex) and metadata. Many users in these new disciplinary formations are new to using complex digital information while others are familiar with creating it but not managing it. These new user communities rely on the professional work of staff working in archives and repositories to make their own research possible.

Lastly, the digital environment changes the legal and policy contexts of access to archives and repositories and archivists must contend with complicated transactions and negotiations to ensure adherence to law. Large scale international projects such as

Europeana (to give one example) reside on a complex network of copyright and intellectual property regimes to make archives available and interoperable. Hacking, privacy, data mining, cybersecurity: these are all not just technical concerns, but arenas where practice and use outpace the legal and policy frameworks to govern them. Other regulations, such as requirements for open access and open data that are being promulgated by national and international funding agencies, make archives and repositories more necessary than ever because publications and research data must be maintained somewhere. However, such mandates are often unfunded ones as archives continue to operate in and justify their existence to financially strapped institutions that are looking for places in their organisations to cut funding.

Archives and access continue to matter, perhaps more than ever. As digital material proliferates and the tools to manipulate it do so as well, what is real and what is false online become difficult to disambiguate. Human rights, scientific research and 'wicked' geopolitical problems (and solving them) rest on accurate and universal access to records and data, whether one is talking about the international crises of forced migration and refugees, human rights, political corruption or climate change.

In short, as the title of the final chapter of this book indicates, even as digital technologies create new opportunities for archives to make new kinds of resources available to users, there are numerous 'archivists' dilemmas'. We continue to look to the archives to maintain our collective memory, a task made more difficult and potentially rewarding with digital access to records. The work of this book is in helping us, the reader, understand how archives and archivists navigate the entanglement of technical, social, organisational and legal challenges that they face daily.

Professor Kalpana Shankar
Head of School of Information & Communication Studies
University College Dublin

Preface

Digital archives: management, use and access participatory approaches in archives

Milena Dobreva

Half of archival collections have no online presence.   (OCLC, 2015, 6)

Welcome to this edited collection of articles exploring digital archives! We live in times when all organisations which collect, preserve and provide access to the collective memory of the humankind – frequently called memory institutions – libraries, archives, museums – are expected to provide digital services. There is a range of driving forces in the process of digitisation, digital curation and providing access to the growing digital collections. One is that diverse collections with descriptions based on different principles originating from the library, museum and archival sectors can be treated as if they are the same in the digital space, especially for hybrid digital resources like Europeana (www.europeana.eu/portal/en). In the long term the process of digitisation may have unexpected consequences for the nature of sector-specific collections description. But is the description of material the only way in which memory sectors are different from other sectors? Or does the transition into digital space require other aspects of the professional trade to be redefined?

Living and working within this period of continuing rapid expansion of accessibility to digital content when the reflection could be very problematic due to the lack of sufficient time distance, calls for understanding what the substantial shifts in the professional phil-osophy, knowledge and practice of digital archives are. This edited collection attempts to explore these uncharted territories. It presents a variety of viewpoints on the archival profession and the drivers of change, and was designed to interest several categories of readers. Archivists will find in the book a breadth of opinions on topics that are changing the archival landscape. Librarians and museum specialists can explore how the digital environment reflects the specific needs of the archival domain, which hopefully will help to strengthen the collaboration and mutual understanding between specialists from these different sectors. Humanities scholars may find useful the discussion of how archival materials enter the territory of digital scholarship. Students can get a generic idea of the range of issues within digital archives. Last but not least, policy makers could explore the relationship between research policies and memory institution policies.

This is not a 'how to create a digital archive' type of book but one that we hope will broaden and deepen the thinking and dialogue between all those academics, professionals and students who are working on different aspects of the digital cultural and scientific heritage.

Maybe you decided to read this book because you work in an archive and are responsible for delivering a digital service. Or maybe you have some knowledge about digital collections and are particularly interested to learn more about accessibility. Or maybe you are a student or a young professional and still expanding your understanding on this domain. Maybe you are moving to the digital world from being a 'traditional' archivist and are exploring what this transition really means. This book is for you all, and we worked to produce a collection which will enrich your understanding of some of the areas that influence the domain of digital archives.

The term *digital archive* can be used in different contexts with a different meaning. In this book we are discussing various aspects of the digital representation of archives, the accumulations of historical records. The term *digital libraries* dominates in the digital world; our aim is to highlight how archivists respond to the specific nature of archival content and services when archives transition into the digital world. The term digital archive can be used to describe a copy of the digital information on a particular electronic device, but we are not discussing the technical aspects of archiving.

The lengthy work on this collection was informed by observations made about the practical needs of archivists who were venturing into the digital world. Between 2012 and 2014 I served as an academic director of a series of summer schools, jointly with Gabriella Ivacs, who at that time was the Chief Archivist of Open Society Archives in Budapest, and since then moved to become the Head of Archives and Records Management at the International Atomic Energy Agency. The summer schools attracted participants from Europe, North America and the Middle East and were delivered by international faculty with various specialisations. They recognised the need to offer supporting reading materials and this collection is a mosaic of chapters prepared mostly by international academics and practitioners who contributed to the series of schools.

Recent developments

The rapid technological changes and the push to provide wide access to cultural and historical holdings are changing the landscape of archives. These processes are highly complex. Aside from the advancement in technical expertise and investment in digitisation it is becoming increasingly imperative to reassess the role and significance of archives and their relationship with citizens.

Archivists – unlike librarians – have traditionally seen themselves as trusted custodians of proprietary records, hence provenance, authenticity and integrity are central to their mission. Archivists have therefore been more reluctant than librarians to take advantage of new digital technologies, which offer less digital content and fewer tools than in the past to enable users to find the resources they require within their collections. The study of primary sources threatens to become the luxury of the few under a new type of digital divide emerging as a new paradox of the seemingly ubiquitous commitment to digital access; this will have important long-term implications on access to knowledge in general.

There have been policy debates in the European Commission in the last few years on issues such as the effect of technological developments on the distribution of and access to audiovisual content, creative works, and participatory approaches in memory institutions. The content of archival collections has been viewed primarily as auxiliary compared with other memory institutions' material. A striking example is when 'archiving' functions – understood in the new technological context for the most part as long-term preservation – are predominantly considered media renewal, migration or emulation, and an intellectual property rights problem, rather than a strategy ensuring the future availability of the content.

Archives are specialised in nature and often of little interest to the average citizen. The archives are still in the early days of identifying and quantifying the economic impact of archives with a first example of establishing a framework for measuring economic impact in archives nation-wide reported in 2012 (see Yakel et al. (2012)). Substantial work still needs to be done to establish the needs in ways of use of digital content in various categories of users. This requires the economic feasibility of needs in digital archival collections to be assessed, and technological barriers examined according to the various needs of diverse user groups. These technological barriers have been amply determined by two European Commission work programmes – the Digital Agenda for Europe launched in 2010 (Digital Agenda 2014) and the Digital Single Market (n.d.). The ambition of introducing a digital single market has its digital cultural heritage dimension too – where the pan-European Europeana, a portal aggregating digital cultural content across Europe, offers in the time of writing close to 60 million objects from some 3500 libraries, museums, archives and galleries. Although there had been substantial developments in this domain, access to cultural heritage collections can still be hindered by the complexity of copyright regulations and licensing procedures.

In line with their public interest missions – such as preservation and provision of cultural and educational access to the records in their collections – archivists of archival institutions have a vested interest in digitising their holdings and making them available online. Some institutions do not own the rights to the works in their possession, but merely hold such records as a function of their role as depositories. For example, it is a major challenge to determine access provisions for orphan works – works to which access is restricted because the copyright holder cannot be traced. The copyright system is still locking away millions of records. For example, Vuopala (2010) states, '21% i.e. 225 000 of the works in European film archives are presumed to be orphan.'

Informed by all these ongoing debates and developments, the series of summer schools we organised in 2012–2014 focused on a number of topics related to digital archives:

- Archives well deserve a separate discussion (rather than being dissolved in generic discussions on digitisation across memory institutions) because of their specialised nature; the access challenges they face are specific to each institution and complex.
- Digitised archival collections and emerging research tools in the digital humanities are not yet well co-ordinated, partly because of the nature of the information. Data is not well classified as copyrighted, orphan or in the public domain. 'Fair dealing' is used sporadically, not systematically, because of issues of classification, and decisions are mostly based on exceptions to copyright law. How can we make sure that we do not lock materials away?
- Questions about research output and raw data supporting research publications need to be addressed with fair dealing, especially because of public funding. In the years following the summer schools, the FAIR data principles had been taken as the guiding principles for research data management (Wilkinson et al., 2016). Making sure digital data are findable, accessible, interoperable and reusable is not trivial and is still an area for raising awareness in the archival communities.
- Archives are rarely top priorities for governmental support; lobby interests are less represented in this domain of cultural heritage where business interests are mostly linked with re-use of material within the cultural and creative interests and their integration in cultural tourism products. Can we compare archives with the publishing industry and publishers, broadcast archives and broadcasters, photo archives and collecting agencies? Is it true that historical archives have less profitable value? Do we have evidential data about market value; are they going to be excluded from the digital single market? What are the implications for access to knowledge, and how are research agendas influenced by this under-representation?

These questions had been reflected in the contributions of our invited lecturers and colleagues from the wider community to this edited collection.

How to read this book

We recommend readers who are not familiar with digital archives to follow the chapters in the order they appear. Readers who are well versed in digital archives may wish to turn to specific chapters on their particular areas of interest.

Contributions to the book elucidate different aspects of the current landscape of digital archives and their management. Part I – 'Drivers for modern digital archives' – sets the scene and offers insights into various aspects of the management of digital archives ranging from research needs to economic and legal matters. Part II, 'Case studies', brings together several examples illustrating specific issues that archivists need to tackle, such as access restrictions, or new trends such as auditing digital archives and engaging citizens to contribute to archive collections.

This edited collection brings together voices of academics and practitioners with various specialisations:

- Enrico Natale (Switzerland) explores the relationship between historians and information professionals against the expanding digital humanities domain.
- Trudy Huskamp Peterson (USA) explores the implications of constant technological changes on the management of archives.
- Guy Pessach (Israel) provides a glimpse into how political economy dimensions started coming into life in the cultural heritage domain in general and archives in particular exploring the economic models and their influence on preserving heritage. While he explores more the initial trends in this area, it is a very informative read which helps to understand current processes of business models and revenue streams in the memory sector.
- Oleksandr Pastukhov (Malta) contributes a range of recommendations that address the legal complexities in digital archives and the general digital cultural heritage domain.
- Carla Basili (Italy) explores the influence of scientific information policies in the European context on the work of all those contributing to the research of the collective memory.
- Pierluigi Feliciati (Italy) studies users' expectations and behaviours when accessing digital archives.

The case studies help to illustrate some of the practical issues in managing digital collections: Elli Papadopoulou, Panayiota Polydoratou, Sotirios Sismanis (Greece) and Donald Tabone (Malta) look at data management in media archives; Gillian Oliver (Australia) looks at access restrictions and their handling; and Milena Dobreva (Bulgaria) and Edel Jennings (Ireland) explore participatory practices.

We do not aim to provide a comprehensive textbook. Digital archives can be imagined as a huge iceberg, and here we suggest several tips that illustrate the complexity of the domain and its relationship with academic and policy domains.

References

Digital Agenda (2014) Digital agenda for Europe,
    http://eige.europa.eu/resources/digital_agenda_en.pdf.
Digital Single Market (n.d.) https://ec.europa.eu/digital-single-market/.
Europeana (n.d.) www.europeana.eu/portal/en.
OCLC (2015) *Making Archival and Special Collections More Accessible*, OCLC
    Research, www.oclc.org/content/dam/research/publications/2015/
    oclcresearch-making-special-collections-accessible-2015.pdf.
Vuopala, A. (2010) *Assessment of the Orphan Works Issue and Costs for Rights
    Clearance*, European Commission, DG Information Society and Media,
    Unit E4 Access to Information, www.ace-film.eu/wp-content/
    uploads/2010/09/Copyright_anna_report-1.pdf.
Wilkinson, M. D., Dumontier, M., Aalbersberg, I. J. et al. (2016) The FAIR
    Guiding Principles for Scientific Data Management and Stewardship,
    Scientific Data, 3, doi:10.1038/sdata.2016.18.
Yakel, E., Duff, W., Tibbo, H., Kriesberg, A. and Cushing, A. (2012) The
    Economic Impact of Archives: surveys of users of government archives in
    Canada and the United States, *The American Archivist*, **75** (2),
    297–325, doi:10.17723/aarc.75.2.002033qg27366gvt.

Acknowledgements

I would like to express my gratitude for the support of Gabriella Ivacs with whom the initial plans of this publication had been discussed. The support of the Summer University programme at the Central European University and Eva Gedeon in particular who helped to manage the first summer school were instrumental for all further activities which led to the production of this book. I would also like to thank Pierluigi Feliciati, who was the local host of the second edition of the summer school Access to Digital Archives in 2013 in Macerata; Hrvoje Stančić from the University of Zagreb, who was the local host of the third summer school; and all faculty and students of the school. Even when they have not contributed to this edited collection, discussions with them helped to shape this book. Last but not least, without the tremendous support of Helen Carley and Natalie Jones from Facet Publishing this work would dissipate into oblivion.

Notes on contributors

Carla Basili is a senior researcher at the Italian National Research Council and Associate Professor of Methodologies of Scientific Information at Sapienza University in Rome; her research focus is on scientific information, information literacy and scientific information policies. She has been Associate Professor of Documentation at the Macerata University (1995–2007) and the Lumsa University in Rome (1998–2008), vice-president of the Italian Association for Advanced Documentation (1998–2004) and Italian delegate in the European Council of Information Associations (1997–2004). Her latest research is on knowledge circulation and scientific information policies. In 2001 Carla Basili initiated and is now the co-ordinator of the European Network on Information Literacy, and she has been the co-ordinator of the European Observatory on Information Literacy Policies and Research since 2006.

Milena Dobreva specialised in digital humanities and digital cultural heritage in the Bulgarian Academy of Sciences where she earned her PhD in 1999 and served as the founding head of the first digitisation centre in Bulgaria (2004). She was also a member on the Executive Board of the National Commission of the United Nations Educational, Scientific and Cultural Organization (UNESCO). In 2007 she was a guest researcher at the University of Glasgow contributing to the DELOS network of excellence in digital libraries. From 2008 to 2011 she worked at the University of Strathclyde in Glasgow and served as the principal investigator for projects in digital preservation and digital libraries funded by the European Commission, Joint Information Systems Committee (JISC), Europeana Foundation and Scottish Funding Council. From 2012 to 2017 Milena was an associate professor at the University of Malta. As a head of the Department of Library Information and Archive Sciences she spearheaded the redesign of the departmental programmes, extended them with a Master's course and supervised the first Maltese Master's graduates in library and information studies. Milena is a member of the editorial board of the journal of the International Federation of Library Associations and Institutions (IFLA), and of the *International Journal on Digital Libraries*.

Pierluigi Feliciati is currently Pro-Rector for Information and Communications Technologies (ICT) and Information Systems at the University of Macerata, where he is Lecturer of Information Science applied to Cultural Heritage and Digital Humanities. He previously co-ordinated the National Archives information system inside the Italian Ministry of Culture. Since the Ministry has been involved in the Minerva European working groups on cultural web quality, his research interests have focused on the quality of users' digital experiences, the management of cultural heritage digital repositories, and on the evaluation of digital library users' behaviour and satisfaction. He served as a technical co-ordinator of the Europeana local project for Italy, the National Archives, and the Marche and Umbria Regional workspaces of the project MICHAEL, and he sat on the boards of the Associazione Italiana Documentazione Avanzata and the Italian Central Institute for Archives.

Edel Jennings is a citizen science and user experience researcher with the Telecommunications Software and Systems Group, Waterford Institute of Technology, Ireland. She co-ordinated the digital humanities citizen science pilot for the EU FP7 project Civic Epistemologies, which involved co-developing digital engagement tools with teenagers and senior citizens to record place-based heritage. Her research interests are in citizen science, the human–computer interaction aspects of crowd sourcing, and social implications of pervasive and social technologies. She led user experience research and evaluation tasks in the EU FP7 project ICT-SOCIETIES, engaging with disaster management, university and enterprise communities to facilitate their experience, reflection and evaluation of novel technologies.

Enrico Natale holds a Master's degree in history and Latin from the University of Geneva and a Master's in political science from University Pompeu Fabra in Barcelona. He is currently a PhD candidate at the University of Basel studying digital history. Enrico Natale has been employed since 2008 by the Swiss Academy for Humanities and Social Sciences as director of infoclio.ch (www.infoclio.ch), the professional portal of historical sciences in Switzerland. In this function he edits a series of digital anthologies (www.livingbooksabouthistory.ch) and an online open-access edition of the complete work of Jean-Jacques Rousseau (rousseauonline.ch). He has published research articles about digital humanities, digital history and documentary (re-)mediations in the digital age.

Gillian Oliver is an associate professor, Caulfield School of Information Technology, at Monash University, Melbourne, Australia. Before joining Monash University she worked at the School of Information Management, Victoria University of Wellington, New Zealand. Her PhD is from Monash University. Her research interests centre on organisational culture, and the influences this has on the way that information is managed. She is the co-author of *Records Management and Information Culture* (Facet Publishing, 2014) and *Digital Curation*, 2nd edition (Facet Publishing, 2016), and the co-editor of *Engaging with Records and Archives* (Facet Publishing, 2016). She is also co-editor in chief of the journal *Archival Science*.

Elli Papadopoulou graduated in library science and information systems at the Technological Education Institute of Thessaloniki, Greece, and received further training in research data management during the first European Data Infrastructure (EUDAT) Summer School. Currently she is involved in the European Open Science Cloud pilot project while also acting as the Greek National Open Access Desk (NOAD) for the needs of OpenAIRE Advance project and as the Greek national node manager for Research Data Alliance project (RDA-4). She has been a volunteer for the Directory of Open Access Journals (DOAJ) since 2015 (associate editor) and is an active member of several resource, description and access groups, particularly promoting the work of the Early Career Engagement Interest Group as one of the co-chairs. Her research interests are open access, open science, FAIR (findable, accessible, interoperable and reusable) research data management, digital preservation and citizen science.

Oleksandr Pastukhov is Senior Lecturer and Information Governance Co-ordinator at the Department of Information Policy and Governance at the University of Malta. He also acts as a deputy co-ordinator of the MAPPING project and a work package leader in the MAPPING, EVIDENCE and CITYCoP projects. He obtained his LLB with a major in private international law from Kiev Taras Shevchenko University in Ukraine (1997), LLM from Northwestern University School of Law in the USA (2000), LLD from Koretsky Institute of State and Law in Ukraine (2003) and PhD in law from the Catholic University of Leuven in Belgium (2008). He spent his post-doctorate years at the Vrije Universiteit Amsterdam in the Netherlands and Strathclyde University in Glasgow, Scotland. Dr Pastukhov is a regular participant and speaker at various national and international fora dedicated to ICT law and policy issues. He is a devoted advocate of privacy, e-governance and media freedom in his native Ukraine and beyond. Dr Pastukhov is the author of a book on digital copyright (*Copyright on the Internet*, Kiev: Shkola, 2004, in Ukrainian language) and over 20 articles or book chapters on diverse legal aspects of ICT use and development, personal data and intellectual property protection online, the introduction of e-government, open and free software development, ISPs' liability and e-commerce taxation. He has also initiated and administered a number of ICT-law-related research, consultancy and training projects in several European countries.

Guy Pessach is a law professor at the Faculty of Law, Hebrew University, Jerusalem, where he is the Academic Director of the Minerva Center for Human Rights. Guy's main areas of research are copyright law, comparative and international aspects of the creative industries and law and technology. Guy was a Fulbright Scholar, Residential Fellow, at the Information Society Project, Yale Law School; a visiting professor at Columbia Law School and the Center for Transnational Legal Studies (Georgetown University Law School); and also an Erasmus Mundus visiting scholar at the Center for Law, Society and Pop Culture, University of Westminster. Before embarking on his academic career, Guy clerked for Justice Zamir at the Israeli Supreme Court.

Trudy Huskamp Peterson is an archival consultant and certified archivist. She holds a PhD in history from the University of Iowa. She spent 24 years with the US National Archives, including more than two years as Acting Archivist of the USA. After retiring from the US government, she was the founding Executive Director of the Open Society Archives in Budapest, Hungary, and then the director of Archives and Records Management for the UN High Commissioner for Refugees. She is a past President of the International Conference of the Round Table on Archives (1993–1995) and the Society of American Archivists (1990–1991), is currently the Chair of the International Council on Archives' Human Rights Working Group and chaired the International Council of Archives (ICA) working group on a standard for access to archives. She consulted the truth commissions in South Africa and Honduras, the Special Court for Sierra Leone, and the Nuclear Claims Tribunal of the Republic of the Marshall Islands, and worked for over three years with the police archives in Guatemala, training the staff in archival processes. Among her many publications are *Final Acts: a guide to preserving the records of truth commissions* (Johns Hopkins University Press, 2005), a study of the records of 20 truth commissions, *Temporary Courts, Permanent Records* (United States Institute of Peace (USIP), 2006), a study of the records of five temporary international criminal courts, and *Securing Police Archives: a Guide for Practitioners* (Swisspeace, 2013), containing advice on managing records of police forces from former repressive regimes.

Panayiota Polydoratou is Assistant Professor at the Department of Library Science and Information Systems at Alexander Technological Educational Institute (ATEI) of Thessaloniki, Greece. She was previously Honorary Visiting Fellow at the Department of Information Science at City University, London, and a member of staff at the Max Planck Digital Library at Max Planck Society, Germany. She holds a PhD in information science from City University, awarded in 2006, and a MSc in information and library studies from the University of Strathclyde. She has previously worked on projects such as the Data Audit Framework and Repository Interface for Overlaid Journal Archives (RIOJA) at University College London. Until 2007, Panayiota was a member of staff at Imperial College London and contributed to projects led by Library Services, such as Defining Image Access. She has also contributed to the Imperial College interim e-theses' project and the VERSIONS project, which was led by London School of Economics. Panayiota's research interests lie in information science, research data management, service units and information provision, new forms of scholarly communication, open access and institutional repositories.

Kalpana Shankar is Professor of Information and Communication Studies and Head of School at University College Dublin's School of Information and Communication Studies. Her research examines how data practices and systems reflect and reify the larger society, culture and institutions where they are enacted. Most recently, she has collaborated with a colleague at the University of Wisconsin-Madison (Professor Kristin Eschenfelder of the School of Library and Information Science) to study sustainability and longevity of social science data archives. She has published and spoken widely on topics related to digital curation, open data and the nature of data and documents.

Sotirios Sismanis is a young information professional originally from Greece where he pursued his studies in the Department of Library Science and Information Systems of the Alexander Technological Educational Institute of Thessaloniki, Greece. During his academic career he was extremely involved in international conferences, research opportunities and writing a book contribution. He is currently based in London.

Donald Tabone was Chief Technology Officer of Allied Newspapers Limited, a major publisher in Malta, providing the necessary strategic direction to meet the company's business requirements. He joined Allied Newspapers Limited after having worked for KPMG and having held various other managerial and hands-on positions across various industries. Donald doubles up as a certified IT trainer and mentor in computer forensics and information security and has delivered several presentations to national entities and private organisations on security-related topics. Currently he is a lecturer with Middlesex University, Malta.

PART I

Drivers for modern digital archives

1

Digital humanities and documentary mediations in the digital age

Enrico Natale

Introduction

Some 25 years after the world wide web was born at the CERN (http://home.web.cern.ch/topics/birth-web) in Geneva in 1993, it should come as no wonder that most of the information we process today is produced and used in digital form. Capable of reproducing most of the pre-existing information carriers such as texts, pictures, sounds and films, the digital format is progressively replacing many of the former media. This process implies there will be profound changes in the daily practices of both scholars in the field of humanities and information professionals.

Understanding changes induced by the influence of digital media within professional practices remains a critical task. As Michel de Certeau reminds us, there is more to learn about the evolution of scientific disciplines through the analysis of the conditions of their production than through their scientific outputs (1975, 65). This chapter proposes to shed light on the current changes of practices within the humanities and to outline several recommendations for a closer collaboration between humanities scholars and information professionals in order to achieve a thoughtful use of digital media.

The first part of the chapter introduces the digital humanities, a field of practices situated at the crossroads between information sciences and the humanities, which has experienced a rapid growth in the past few years. It discusses the origins and scope of digital humanities, as well as the question of its definition. The close association between digital humanities and information sciences is also highlighted.

The second part shifts the focus from digital practices to professional collaborations and analyses the evolving relationship between researchers and information professionals under the influence of digital information systems. Recent changes in the use of libraries and archives are discussed, drawing from recent surveys about information practices among humanities scholars.

Finally, in the third part are recommendations on how to improve this relationship in a digital environment. It draws on previous points in order to propose some ways to introduce a closer collaboration between information professionals and humanities scholars within the context of the digital information landscape. In particular, it advocates the benefits of enhancing the visibility of documentary mediations in online environments.

The rise of the digital humanities

From humanities computing to digital humanities

The use of computers in the humanities is usually traced back to 1949, when Roberto Busa, a Jesuit priest, started a project to build a general concordance of the work of St Thomas Aquinas. He succeeded in convincing Thomas J. Watson, co-founder of IBM, to provide the computing machines to process the text. The project started in the suburbs of Rome, along with dozens of young women recruited to encode the Latin text into punched cards to be processed by IBM computers (Terras, 2013a). The work went on for 30 years and resulted in 50 printed volumes of concordance indexes in the 1970s, a CD-ROM edition in the 1990s and a web-based version released in 2005 (see Corpus Thomisticum; www.corpusthomisticum.org/). This project can be considered the forerunner of successive initiatives using computational methods to analyse textual corpuses. Focusing on corpus creation, text encoding and computational analysis of texts, this type of research forms the core of a discipline called humanities computing, which was formalised from the 1970s onwards, mainly within the field of classical studies, linguistic and literature. The Association for Computers and the Humanities was created in 1973, the Association for Literary and Linguistic Computing in 1978.

In 1987 the Text Encoding Initiative (TEI; www.tei-c.org/) appeared, which is considered one of the major scholarly initiatives in dealing with text within digital environments (Ide and Sperberg-McQueen, 1995). TEI is a set of XML-based internationally recognised and periodically updated rules for encoding text. TEI-encoded texts are machine-readable and therefore qualify for computational analysis and for the preparation of digital editions.

From the late 1960s onward, historians also started to use computers to experiment with quantitative methods of analysis. In France, this trend was best represented by a group of economic and social historians gathered around the journal *Annales*. These historians were interested in using new types of historical sources such as census data and other serial documents that required quantitative methods to be processed. In 1968, Emmanuel Le Roy Ladurie, an eminent representative of this quantitative turn, wrote the following statement: 'The historian of tomorrow will be a programmer or won't be at all' (Le Roy Ladurie, 1968).

The spread of personal computers during the 1980s further accelerated the technological transition. Promoted by massive advertisement campaigns,[1] personal computers entered the workplaces and homes of middle-class families. As computers became ubiquitous in cultural and social discourse, the general public learned that they were not only calculating machines, but also versatile tools that could be used for a variety of purposes. Computers could be used both for work and for leisure and were capable of handling not only numbers, but also texts, images, music and films (Turkle, 1984).

The propagation of office software during the 1990s transformed the everyday practices of many practitioners. Along with early digital networks emerged electronic mail, which in turn rapidly changed professional communication habits. The world wide web, whose use began to spread among the general public in Europe around 1995, propelled the transition of information towards the digital format.

At this point, it became clear that digital media represented an epochal turn in the production, access and use of information, whose effects on the humanities were far more significant than initially predicted. When in the early 2000s the designation 'digital humanities' replaced the term 'humanities computing' used since the 1970s, it marked this new awareness of the far-reaching consequences of digital technologies on the humanities (Clivaz, 2012).

Defining the digital humanities

The name 'digital humanities' appeared for the first time in 2001 during the preparatory work for the *Companion to Digital Humanities*, a collective work published by Blackwell Editions in 2004 (Kirschenbaum, 2010). In 2002, the Alliance of Digital Humanities Organizations was born in Tubingen, thanks to a collaboration between the Association for Computers in the Humanities and the Association for Literary and Linguistic Computing.

As it appears in a special journal issue dedicated to controversies around digital humanities and in other recent literature (Gold, 2012; Thaller, 2012), the digital humanities research programme does not have a unified definition, but a consensus exists among existing opinions. According to a Southampton University participant of the Day of Digital Humanities – an online initiative that gathers the practitioners of the field once per year: 'I see "Digital Humanities" as an umbrella term for two different but related developments: 1) Humanities Computing (the specialist use of computing technology to undertake humanities research) and 2) the implications for the humanities of the social revolution created by ubiquitous computing and online access' (TAPoR at Alberta Wiki, 2011). A similar definition was proposed by a researcher from California State University: 'Digital Humanities is a combination of using computer technologies to study human cultures and studying the effect of computer technologies on human cultures' (TAPoR at Alberta Wiki, 2011).

Yet other constituents bring the digital humanities community together. A first common thread is the desire to fill the gap between theory and practice within the humanities by embedding the practical aspects of building tools and digital collections into the epistemological perspective of knowledge production. Another trend is the commitment to produce research that can generate interest in the general public beyond the walls of the university. Related to this point, digital humanities practitioners share widespread support in favour of the free sharing of knowledge and for legal solutions allowing the free circulation of information like open licences and Creative Commons licences. Last but not least, the notion of transdisciplinarity is central to the digital humanities, stressing the importance of collaboration between computer sciences, information sciences and the humanities.

The major journals published in this field are *Digital Scholarship in the Humanities* (Association for Linguistic and Literary Computing, 1986–), *Digital Humanities Quarterly* (Alliance of Digital Humanities Organization, 2007–) and *Digital Studies/Le Champ numérique* (Society for Digital Humanities, 2008–). In less than a decade, centres committed to digital humanities have multiplied throughout the world. See the Alliance of Digital Humanities Organizations (http://adho.org/) for a list of more than 200 digital humanities institutions worldwide. In the USA, the *National Endowment for the Humanities*, a public institution responsible for funding research in the humanities, opened its Office of Digital Humanities in 2006. In England, King's College London (KCL) and University College London (UCL) have opened centres for digital humanities. See www.kcl.ac.uk/artshums/depts/ddh/index.aspx (KCL) and www.ucl.ac.uk/dh/ (UCL). Today, Germany alone counts a dozen of master programmes in digital humanities. See Studium und Lehre in Digital Humanities Deutschland (www.dig-hum.de/studienstandorte).

A special relationship with information sciences

Recently, the link between the digital humanities and librarianship has been strengthened. A special section was created within the American Librarian Association in 2012 (http://acrl.ala.org/dh/) and several journals released special issues on the topic (e.g. Rockenbach et al., 2013). In fact, several digital humanities centres are located in university libraries,[2] and conversely several public libraries host digital research labs.[3]

There has been a renewed research interest for the material forms and the social context in which knowledge production is embedded, both nowadays and in the past. Knowledge institutions and emblematic figures of information science, such as Paul Otlet, have recently been the object of a number of research projects, such as *Les lieux de savoir* by the French historian Christian Jacob (2007; 2011; see also Rayward, 2008; Wright, 2014).

Moreover, epistemological reflections on the effects of digital technologies on scholarly outputs are on the rise (see Berry, 2012; Gold, 2012). They present interesting similarities with what has occurred over two decades in libraries and archives as a consequence of the digitisation of catalogues and finding aids. Those reflexive fields of inquiries offer a fruitful common ground of collaboration for humanities scholars and information professionals.

Finally, almost every digital humanities project involves informational skills – whether to publish source documents online or to build a research database – that call for a closer collaboration with information professionals. As a librarian recently explained, digital humanities projects involve archival collections, copyright and fair use questions, information organisation, emerging technologies and progressive ideas about the role of text(s) in society, all potential areas of expertise within the field of librarianship (Vandegrift, 2012).

The evolving relationship between historians and information professionals

The increasing gap between scholars and information professionals

Commenting on a survey on the changing research practices among historians, the director of the American Historical Association stated in 2013: 'Historians are increasingly isolated from the professionals who have traditionally supported their work' (Townsend, 2013). Indeed, many recent surveys confirm that scholars, regardless of the differences between disciplines and education levels, tend to go to the library in person less and less often (Bulger et al., 2011). Most of them frequently use online databases and electronic journals – to which access is provided by the library – and search for content by running simple keyword queries. A similar observation applies to archives. Historians visit archives for shorter and shorter periods, using them first and foremost to produce digital photographs of archival material to be studied later (Schonfeld and Rutner, 2012, 8). Furthermore, research that is grounded in the detailed study of specific archival collections tends to give way to thematic research using heterogeneous sources.[4] In both cases the direct collaboration between researchers and information professionals falls short, while the digital mediations become increasingly important.

Changing information practices

One of the most significant and documented changes in scientific practices concerns the search for information. The computerisation of library catalogues and the subsequent proliferation of bibliographic databases have enabled scholars to use IT tools for their information needs since the end of the 1980s. After the invention of the world wide web in the 1990s, what could be found online was no longer limited to catalogues and finding aids, but included a significant part of the scientific literature and countless collections of digitised documents.

The development of full-text search engines facilitated the search for information online and established the web as a universal container of information. John Battelle in his book *The Search* (2005) described how the growing use of search engines and the similarities in internet search tools had a disrupting influence on documentation practices. One major change is the advent of online browsing. As Stephen Ramsay (2010) puts it: 'The question is whether we are ready to accept surfing and stumbling – screwing around, broadly understood – as a research methodology.'

This trend was confirmed by a survey from the UK in 2008, which showed that the younger generation demonstrated a 'skimming and bouncing' search behaviour, which started for 90% of the interviewees directly on the web via a generic search engine (Rowlands et al., 2008). The time spent on each resource was very short, and in the course of the search a succession of very different resources were visited, while little attention was given to their results. Young researchers moved steadily from one source to another, clicked extensively on hyperlinks, and spent little time evaluating the relevance of each source. In fact, the study revealed that young people spent as much time searching for information as reading the information they found.[5] Further studies of David Nicholas (from 2010 and 2014) confirmed these observations.

This cross-sectional search drastically contrasts with the hierarchical structure of information, particularly in libraries and archives. Search engines have the effect of flattening the organisational structure of information, which becomes in the long run more and more invisible to researchers.

This is of course an illusion. Every search engine follows a specific organisational pattern, from which it cannot divert. Page Rank, for instance, the search algorithm of Google, although very complex, is based on the academic citation system, explains Matteo Pasquinelli (2009): 'Academic citation literature has been applied to the web, largely by counting citations or backlinks to a given page. This gives some approximation of a page's importance or quality.' Unfortunately, the operating process of search engines remains a black box for most users.

The Google paradox: higher expectations, less visibility

Another paradox related to users' expectations is consequential to the generalisation of web search engines. As a consequence of the computing power of modern computers, the duration of a search query comes close to zero. Moreover, search results are over-abundant, giving the impression that a wealth of information is always available, regardless of its source. These facts alter users' expectations; users become accustomed to having immediate and unlimited online access to information.

This overload of information distracts researchers from the fact that what is available online is only a small fraction of existing information. Most knowledge – which is not and will never be available in digital form – is sentenced to a new form of invisibility because of the reliance on online instant access.

This creates a paradoxical tension between the ease of access to digital information and its incomplete nature. Some surveyed researchers even claim that 'If it's not online, it doesn't exist, and it's not important' (Harley et al., 2010, 18). As a reaction to this new type of prejudice, several historians 'expressed concerns about selective digitisation, and the risk that digital archives may bias historical scholarship towards more readily accessible archival materials' (Harley et al., 2010, 481).

A broader information ecosystem

Fortunately, most humanities scholars do not share such radical opinions and continue to use traditional search methods to meet their information needs. The vast majority of researchers carry out traditional bibliographic searches, follow the chain of references from a publication to another, and still actively participate in academic conferences (Bulger et al., 2011, 68). Nevertheless, humanities scholars have adopted a series of digital information practices, in addition to traditional research methods. Some authors describe this evolution as a 'broadening of their information ecosystem' (Bulger et al., 2011, 65).

Contemporary practices are mostly based on a combination of analogue and digital tools. A survey carried out among American historians in 2012 acknowledges that 'nearly all of the interviewees had some combination of paper and digital notes' (Schonfeld and Rutner, 2012, 26) and that 'in many cases scholars used both print and electronic version[s] of a single text during a research project' (Schonfeld and Rutner, 2012, 19). This also applies to how digital tools are used in archives; the search of archival sources through online finding aids or digital sources repositories does not replace a visit to the archives, but rather precedes and prepares it. Thus, we should think of digital media as being integrated with and complementary to analogue tools, rather than substituting them.

Making visible documentary mediation

Considering the above mentioned points, a major challenge for archivists and librarians is to maintain the visibility of their documentary mediations, especially online. What follows are some thoughts from the point of view of a humanities scholar on how a closer collaboration could be fostered between information specialists and humanities researchers in the digital age.

First, I would like to share an assumption about the centrality of cultural heritage institutions in the digital information landscape. Libraries and archives existed long before digital technologies transformed the way by which information is produced and shared. Until today, they remain the bedrock of the knowledge infrastructure of Western modernity. When Google turned to academic libraries to digitise their books, it was not out of intellectual curiosity, but because their algorithms drastically needed content in massive amounts to grow smarter. Put simply, computation power and processing capacities are worthless without a meaningful input.

The fact that archives and libraries are the keepers of the cultural heritage is not likely to change in the near future. With the rise of the digital information society, they are adapting to new formats and new information consumption patterns as they have already done in the past. But they will nevertheless continue to be key institutions providing knowledge as well as historical evidence. One could envision cultural heritage institutions as the foundations that support the edifice of Western knowledge, with the internet as a new layer, placed on top of them, which allows instant duplication and sharing of their contents.

Librarians and archivists should venture into the digital world with this self-confidence. They should trust their own expertise in collecting, preserving and providing future generations with access to knowledge, while accepting the idea of releasing digital copies of their documents over the internet, beyond any possibility of control, although this breaches their historical practices.

This may appear as an ideal statement. In reality, sharing possibilities are constrained by financial resources, technological know-how, legal copyright frameworks, and the balance of power between interested parties. Indeed, cultural heritage institutions are faced with a number of threats, notably related to the issue of copyright regimes for digital content. Restrictive copyright rules are in many cases impeding librarians and archivists from sharing their holdings over the internet. In this area, librarians and archivists find themselves at the forefront of the global struggle for knowledge dissemination and are doing their best to defend their positions within international fora such as the lobbying activities of IFLA (www.ifla.org/clm) and The Internet Commerce Association (ICA) at the World Intellectual Property Organization.

Online presence

The first step for libraries and archives to secure a good online visibility is to worry about their online presence. Building a good website that gives access to several finding aids, with an effective search function, constitutes an essential step that most archivists and librarians have already taken. Another step is to be present on popular social networks, like Facebook and Twitter, so as to meet the digital social habits of their users (Charnigo and Barnett-Ellis, 2007; see also the Facebook group Librarians and Facebook, which has almost 2000 members).

Recent surveys about search practices have shown that many users start their search on the web rather than on their library website. As a consequence, users are most likely to reach libraries and archives websites during the course of a general search on the web. This calls for strategies in search engine optimisation, in order to maximise the chances for libraries and archives to bring their content to their users online. For instance, when building a digital collection or an online finding aid, one should make sure that every single record has its own stable URL, which can be found via online search engines without having to go through the library website. Although most recent professional computer programs already have those functions embedded, it is helpful to keep those issues in mind while setting an online communication agenda.

Crowd sourcing is another popular topic for cultural heritage institutions trying to strengthen their online communication. Several institutions have placed documents on interactive media platforms and invited users to describe images or give them keywords (see www.flickr.com/commons). Crowd-sourcing projects are very diverse, including identifying and tagging photographs, transcribing archival sources, and geo-referencing documents (Holley, 2010; Noll, 2012; Oomen and Aroyo, 2011).

According to Melissa Terras, head of the project Transcribe Bentham (http://blogs.ucl.ac.uk/transcribe-bentham/), what is really at stake with crowd sourcing is not harvesting the 'wisdom of the crowds' but rather to find the few exceptionally skilled and enthusiastic users who will make a difference in getting the work done, so calling for public participation is more effective as an online communication strategy than for collaborative research (Terras, 2013b). Crowd-sourcing projects often go hand in hand with a 'gamification' facet where computer games are developed to involve users in tasks which help to add or refine digital cultural heritage content. Games provide users with incentives to keep supplying free labour (De Kosnik, n.d.; Terranova, 2003).

Content in digital form

Delivering content in digital formats adapted to computational research and online publishing practices is another emerging field of interest for libraries and archives. At a basic level, this involves implementing stable identifiers for digital references and documents

– like URLs, digital object identifiers and other technologies – which allow digital sources to be cited in a clear and sustainable way. See the abundant literature about digital objects identification, for example, Younger (1997).

At a more advanced stage, cultural heritage institutions could consider the opportunity to offer selected contents in machine-readable formats for users who are interested to process them further computationally. Possible initiatives include making digital collections and their metadata downloadable in appropriate formats or making quantitative or serial data available as spreadsheets. Downloadable geographic co-ordinates are also of interest for scholars working with geographical information systems.

These suggestions are in line with the open data movement, which advocates for online availability of data produced by public institutions. A branch of the open data movement deals explicitly with cultural knowledge institutions (see OpenGLAM; http://openglam. org/). Following this trend, the Swiss National Library released in 2012 its Swiss National Bibliography in MARC-XML format under a Creative Commons licence, allowing any interested person to download the data (http://opac.admin.ch/cgi-bin/ nboai/VTLS/Vortex. pl?verb=ListRecords&set=sb&metadataPrefix=marcxml).

Furthermore, as libraries and archives will inevitably be keeping more and more documents in digital form in the future, there will be a need for new finding aids to explore the contents of the documents. The technologies of text mining, semantic linking and network analysis and their implementation to run complex queries in vast amounts of documents could well become an integral part of library and archives services in the next decades.

Information literacy

It has been a traditional role for libraries and archives to help their users to become more effective information consumers, by teaching them first how to recognise their information needs and then to locate and eventually use information sources effectively.

The complexity of the information landscape has increased considerably in the 20th century. In addition to book and print media, a variety of other information formats have become mainstream, which still require specific literacies in order to be correctly interpreted. This situation has become even more critical since the rise of the world wide web, as the features of digital media are constantly evolving.

Historians have recently acknowledged an increasing need for support in order to deal with the various types of historical sources. A survey among historians in 2012 revealed that 'PhD students reported significant uncertainty about their knowledge of research practices' (Schonfeld and Rutner, 2012), forcing the President of the American Historical Association to admit that 'the experience of learning to work with primary source – which is at the heart of the historical method – can be described as informal, at best' (Townsend, 2013).

In a digital media landscape dominated by global profit concerns, critical perspectives from the viewpoint of information specialists are badly needed. Coates (2013, 149) suggests librarians should inform users about e-books: 'since the adoption of a standardised set of features is unlikely in the near future, librarians can increase researchers' understanding of the benefits and drawbacks of e-books through educational programs and individual consultations'.

There are two sets of insights that libraries and archives could share with researchers. A first set relates to the specific material characteristics of individual media: What are their material forms, their technical properties? What legal framework are they imbedded in? What are the challenges for their preservation? A second set of insights – the object of the next section – relates to the documentary mediations the documents go through within cultural heritage institutions.

Making explicit documentary mediations

At the turn of the 21st century, many commentators stated that the internet had opened an 'age of disintermediation', where commodities, financial products and information would flow directly from the producers to users, therefore making traditional intermediaries useless (Espaignet, Ramatoulaye and Laurenceau, 2003). Ten years later, although digital networks challenged the previous *status quo* in many domains, the 'age of disintermediation' proved to a large extent to be an illusion (Papy and Leblond, 2009).

On the contrary, the exponential growth of information accessible through the internet calls more than ever for filters to sort out relevant and authoritative sources among the massive amount of available content. Like information brokers, libraries and archives could favourably promote their traditional skills in this context by making explicit the documentary mediation they are performing.

This would contribute to the denaturalisation of information retrieval by raising users' awareness about the diversity and complexity of documentary mediations. For example, it would benefit users to be reminded that a query in a search engine implies a number of selection steps that ought to be understood. By making explicit the documentary mediations they perform – both analogue and digital – libraries and archives would thus contribute to raising the general level of information literacy of their users, while reasserting their traditional role as competence centres for knowledge management.

More specifically, archivists and librarians should publish more about their administrative procedures and make them transparent. The choice of an ontology, a classification system or an inventory structure influences the way researchers access materials, so they ought to be made explicit. Similarly, the source of descriptions and additional contextual information added to the records should be transparent. What information was obtained based on the evidence in the actual sources (from legacy) and what was subsequently added by information professionals?

This is especially important for collections of documents that are available online. According to what criteria were they selected? What portion of the total holdings do they represent? Do they come from a single record group or from a multiplicity of provenances? What additional information is being provided? All those issues inform users about the documents they are using and the constitution of documentary mediations.

Even subject terminologies used to qualify information such as the Dewey Decimal Classification or the Universal Decimal Classification might prejudice the way in which information is accessed. To prevent such bias to go unnoticed, it would be useful to make their origins and limitations explicit. This also applies, although in different terms, to modern subject terminologies like the Library of Congress Subject Headings or the French *Répertoire d'autorité-matière encyclopédique et alphabétique unifié* (RAMEAU; http://rameau.bnf.fr/).

Conclusion

The expansion of the digital cultural content has the potential for initiating tighter collaboration between humanities researchers and information professionals. Historians and information specialists need to update their professional skills in order to cope with the digital environment, and they should go down this path together.

Digital humanities offers a common ground to achieve this task. As an interdisciplinary field of practices, it provides the framework to bring together the skills of information professionals with the methods of humanities scholars. Thus, the field could constitute a privileged common space for a thoughtful implementation of digital technologies and a critical reflection about them.

There are many challenges ahead. Forms of digital publications are rapidly developing, opening new possibilities for innovative scholarly narratives that integrate source documents and do not rely solely on text. Digital networks offer new perspectives for collaborative research. Document collections that are disseminated among several institutions can now be digitally reunited, while historians living far from each other can work together in virtual environments. A variety of digital tools can drastically extend the scope of research by managing vast amounts of information or by running content analysis in large collections.

But every opportunity comes with risks. In the global power struggle for information control that is taking place today, the information sciences and humanities could well lose their role as keepers of knowledge to the benefit of the commercial interests of the technology industry. By combining their efforts, scholars and information professionals would increase their chance to develop a strong expertise enabling them to get the best of the fast-developing digital toolbox and to use it critically.

Notes

1 See for instance the advertising clip made by Ridley Scott for Apple Computers in 1983 (Scott, 1983).
2 See for instance the Scholars' Lab in the University of Virginia Library or the Emory Centre for Digital Scholarship in the Robert W. Woodruff Library.

3 See for instance the New York Public Library labs or the British Library labs.
4 Oral interview with Urs Kalin, Swiss Social Archives, Zürich, 2013.
5 According to the authors of this study many of these information behaviours pre-date the web. Their origins may go back to the 1980s and to the influence of television, video games and music in digital form (Rowlands et al., 2008).

References

Battelle, J. (2005) *The Search: how Google and its rivals rewrote the rules of business and transformed our culture*, Portfolio, 5–17.

Berry, D. M. (ed.) (2012) *Understanding Digital Humanities*, Palgrave Macmillan.

Bulger, M., Meyer, E. T., de la Flor, G., Terras, M., Wyatt, S., Jirotka, M., Eccles, K. and Madsen, C. (2011) *Reinventing Research? Information practices in the humanities, a Research Information Network report*, www.rin.ac.uk/system/files/attachments/Humanities_Case_Studies_for_screen_2_0.pdf.

Charnigo, L. and Barnett-Ellis, P. (2007) Checking Out Facebook.com: the impact of a digital trend on academic libraries, *Information Technology and Libraries*, **26** (1), 23–34.

Clivaz, C. (2012) The Next Era or Common Era 2.0: reading digital culture since antiquity and modernity, in Clivaz, C., Meizoz, J., Vallotton, F. and Verheyden, J. (eds), *Lire Demain: des manuscrits antiques à l'ère digitale [Reading Tomorrow: from ancient manuscripts to the digital age]*, Presses polytechniques et universitaires romandes, 23–60.

Coates, H. (2013) Academic Historians in Canada Report Both Positive and Negative Attitudes Towards E-books for Teaching and Research, *Evidence Based Library and Information Practice*, **8** (4), 148–50.

De Certeau, M. (1975) *L'écriture de l'histoire*, Paris, Gallmard.

De Kosnik, A. (n.d.) Interrogating 'Free' Fan Labor, Spreadable Media, http://spreadablemedia.org/essays/kosnik/#.Us1ZxPaBDFd.

Espaignet, S., Ramatoulaye, F. and Laurenceau, A. (2003) *Pertinence de l'Idée de Désintermédiation Documentaire: rapport de recherche*, École Nationale Supérieure des Sciences de l'Information et des Bibliothèques.

Gold, M. K. (2012) *Debates in the Digital Humanities*, University of Minnesota Press.

Harley, Di., Acord, S. K., Earl-Novell, S., Lawrence, S. and King, C. J. (2010) *Assessing the Future Landscape of Scholarly Communication: an exploration of faculty values and needs in seven disciplines,* UC Berkeley: Center for Studies in Higher Education, https://escholarship.org/uc/item/15x7385g.

Holley, R. (2010) Crowdsourcing: how and why should libraries do it?, *D-Lib Magazine,* **16** (3).

Ide, N. M. and Sperberg-McQueen, C. (1995) The TEI: history, goals, and future, *Computers and the Humanities,* **29** (1), 5–15.

Jacob, C. (ed.) (2007) *Lieux de Savoir: espaces et communautés,* Paris, Albin Michel.

Jacob, C. (ed.) (2011) *Lieux de Savoir: les mains de l'intellect,* Paris, Albin Michel.

Kirschenbaum, M. G. (2010) What is Digital Humanities and What's it Doing in English Departments?, *ADE Bulletin,* no. 150.

Le Roy Ladurie, E. (1968) La Fin des Érudits, *Le Nouvel Observateur,* 8 May.

Nicholas, D. (2010) The Behaviour of the Researcher of the Future (the 'Google generation'), *Art Libraries Journal,* **35** (1), 18–21.

Nicholas, D. (2014) The Google Generation, the Mobile Phone and the 'Library' of the Future: implications for society, governments and libraries, in A. Noorhidawati et al. (eds) ICOLIS-2014, Kuala-Lumpur DLIS, FCSIT, 2014: 1–8.

Noll, A. G. (2012) *Crowdsourcing Transcriptions of Archival Materials,* History Department, University of Massachusetts Boston, https://scholarworks.umb.edu/cgi/viewcontent.cgi?article=1062&context =ghc.

Oomen, J. and Aroyo, L. (2011) Crowdsourcing in the Cultural Heritage Domain: opportunities and challenges, in *Proceedings of the 5th International Conference on Communities and Technologies,* 138–49.

Papy, F. and Leblond, C. (2009) Bibliothèques Numériques: la nécessaire médiation, *Communication et langages,* 161, 37–57.

Pasquinelli, M. (2009) Google's PageRank Algorithm: a diagram of cognitive capitalism and the rentier of the common intellect, in Becker, K., Stalder, F. (eds), *Deep Search,* Transaction Publishers, http://matteopasquinelli.com/google-pagerank-algorithm/.

RAMEAU (n.d.) Répertoire d'autorité-matière encyclopédique et alphabétique unifié, http://rameau.bnf.fr/.

Ramsay, S. (2010) The Hermeneutics of Screwing Around; or what you do with a million books, unpublished presentation delivered at Brown University.

Rayward, W. B. (2008) *European Modernism and the Information Society*, Ashgate.

Rockenbach, B. et al. (2013) Digital Humanities in Libraries: new models for scholarly engagement, *Journal of Library Administration*, **53** (1), 10–26.

Rowlands, I., Nicholas, D., Williams, P., Huntington, P., Fieldhouse, M., Gunter, B., Withey, R., Jamali, H. R., Dobrowolski, T. and Tenopir, C. (2008) The Google Generation: the information behaviour of the researcher of the future, *Aslib Proceedings: New Information Perspectives*, **60** (4), 290–310, http://emeraldinsight.com/0001-253X.htm.

Schonfeld, R. C. and Rutner, J. (2012) *Supporting the Changing Research Practices of Historians*, Ithaka S+R, www.sr.ithaka.org/wp-content/mig/reports/supporting-the-changing-research-practices-of-historians.pdf.

Scott, R. (1983) Apple Keynote: the '1984' ad introduction, YouTube, www.youtube.com/watch?v=lSiQA6KKyJo.

TAPoR at Alberta Wiki (2011) How Do You Define Digital Humanities?, www.artsrn.ualberta.ca/taporwiki/index.php/How_do_you_define_Humanities_Computing_/_Digital_Humanities%3F.

Terranova, T. (2003) Free Labor: producing culture for the digital economy, *Electronic Book Review*, 20 June, www.electronicbookreview.com/thread/technocapitalism/voluntary.

Terras, M. (2013a) For Ada Lovelace Day: Father Busa's female punch card operatives, Melissa Terras' blog, 15 October, http://melissaterras.blogspot.ch/2013/10/for-ada-lovelace-day-father-busas.html.

Terras, M. (2013b) The Importance of Others: using digital humanities to involve a wide audience in cultural heritage, lecture at the University of Lausanne, 23 June.

Thaller, M. (ed.) (2012) Controversies around the Digital Humanities, *Historical Social Research*, **37** (3), 376pp.

Townsend, R. B. (2013) Report Claims History Discipline Failing in Modern Research Practices, *Perspectives on History*, www.historians.org/publications-and-directories/perspectives-on-history/february-2013/report-claims-history-discipline-failing-in-modern-research-practices.

Turkle, S. (1984) *The Second Self: computers and the human spirit*, Simon & Schuster.

Vandegrift, M. (2012) What Is Digital Humanities and What's It Doing in the Library?, *In The Library with the Leadpipe*, 27 June, www.inthelibrarywiththeleadpipe.org/2012/dhandthelib/.

Wright, A. (2014) *Cataloging the World: Paul Otlet and the birth of the information age*, Oxford University Press.

Younger, J. A. (1997) Resources Description in the Digital Age, *Library Trends*, **45** (3), 462–81.

2

Managing turbulence

Trudy Huskamp Peterson

Introduction

Managing is getting things done through people. In the 1980s, the mantra was 'management by walking around', the idea that a manager who wandered through the workplace, observing people and equipment and working conditions, would encourage better performance and productivity. When a mechanical system – say, a digital one – is introduced between the manager and the people within the organisation, things change.

Managing in an archival organisation where some of the materials are digital is one aspect of the greater management realm. Using digital tools while managing people who work in the archives is another. How does the advent of the digital ecosystem in archives change the composition of the workforce that makes up the archival service? How does it change the management of staff? And how does it change the characteristics of managers?

First we will take a close look at hiring as an example of how thoroughly digital systems have captured a fundamental managerial responsibility. Then we will pull back to a wider view to see where staff members work and the electronic tools that are available to managers for supervision. Next we turn to the nature of the workforce itself and the changes that are possible by choosing digital management options. Finally, we will look at the characteristics of archival leaders in an organisation that depends on digital systems.

Hiring as an example of digital process

When a manager decides to hire, the first step is recruitment. Today that nearly always includes electronic distribution of the job vacancy announcement. Although there is no single site for posting archives vacancies worldwide, governments have electronic sites where jobs are posted, some archival associations have electronic job sites, and archival listservs also post jobs (such as the listservs of the International Council on Archives and ARMA [Association of Records Managers and Administrators] International). The Society of American Archivists (SAA) boasts to employers that posting with the SAA online ensures that they will 'find the best', 'meet their recruitment goals and attract top talent.'

Once the employers have the applications in hand (virtually), they can review not only the application but also the candidate's social media profile. Although Facebook, for example, says in its terms of service that an account holder 'will not share your password', many social media accounts are not protected by a password and can easily be viewed by a prospective employer. How much weight the hiring official gives to the social media information will vary by employer and information. But employers who use it in decision making need to figure out how to document the social media account that was considered in the hiring decision. In some institutions and governments, photographs are not permitted on employment applications to reduce the risk of discrimination on grounds of race, gender, age and so forth. Use of social media to gain information about prospective employees undercuts that restriction; for further discussion, see Quast (2012).

Employment interviews were once face-to-face meetings; they then became telephone interviews, but now are often conducted on Skype or other computer-assisted software. The prospect of unfairness in such distance interviews led the American Historical Association to issue guidelines for telephone and video interviews (American Historical Association, 2011).

Once the manager selects the candidate for the job, the new hire may be informed by e-mail or text, and the contract may be sent to her as an e-mail attachment. Some institutions still require a signature and the return of a signed paper, while others accept a scanned image of the page that has been printed and signed (few accept electronic signatures – yet).

All that is left is to agree on is the means of paying the salary. Some institutions require that all salaries be deposited electronically, many provide that as an option, and payment in cash is almost non-existent except in countries with failing or unreformed banking systems. For example, the World Bank is actively working with countries to install electronic accounting and payroll systems for government employees; see the various 2013 projects in Africa (World Bank, 2013). As a general practice in many countries, newly hired employees provide their banking information to the employer and then trust that credits will show up regularly in their bank account.

In sum, at every step of the process, from advertising to payment, the tool used is digital. The electronic penetration of hiring, like most management processes, is complete.

Where we work: the impact of digital systems

Digital tools allow management to supervise staff members who are working in a different building, area or even country. More and more people are able to work at a distance (known as the flexible place option, 'flexiplace', 'telework' or 'telecommuting'), even if carrying out archival functions.

Look at archival appraisal as a function. In the pre-digital world, the appraisal archivist usually went to the records creator, looked at the records (or, often, a sample of them), and made a decision. Managers worried about the expense of sending appraisers to the creating institutions and the cost of shipping and storing quantities of records, but with digital systems, if the archivist has permission to access the creator's electronic system, records can be appraised anywhere, and the selected records can be 'ingested' into the archives digitally, too.

Similarly, look at archival description. When archivists review and describe paper records, still photographs, video tapes and other traditional formats, they have to be located where the materials are. If the records are digital, it is possible to work from other locations, so long as the electronic connectivity has robust security. Some institutions routinely send electronic instructions through open commercial electronic systems. However, many institutions do not permit staff members to work with digital materials that are security classified or otherwise restricted except in facilities that have protected firewalls (not in a home, for instance).

Even archival reference service may be susceptible to flexiplace. If the service consists of locating and retrieving information electronically and changing permissions to allow a requester to see it or posting it to an open site, this can be done from any location where connectivity is available. However, as long as archives have masses of records that are not in electronic formats, few reference staff members will be able to work at a distance, but increasingly it is an option for a part of the reference workforce.

For all its advantages, flexiplace poses management challenges. First of all, interpersonal relationships are still a vital part of management. But if an item is appraised in Ottawa and described in Chennai, and the reference service in Budapest, how does the manager develop working relationships with the people carrying out the functions? Large archival organisations have for many decades had dispersed archival locations, from the four locations managed by the archives service of the French train system (Société nationale des chemins de fer français; SNCF) to the 40-plus locations administered by the US National Archives and Records Service. In these organisations managers make efforts to meet the people in the work units. If archival work is spread over the globe, this will be less feasible – or greatly more expensive.

Second, the manager has to use electronic tools to monitor work done at a distance. Managers have always had to balance between the rights of the employer and the rights of the employee while supervising work (see Beesley, 2016). For years telephones have been monitored (or employers at least had the option to monitor calls made by staff members), but the use of personal mobile phones and the increasing acceptance of flexiplace has greatly lessened the efficacy of this kind of monitoring. Today, however, monitoring computer use by employees is very common, although once again off-site work on personal equipment is nearly impossible to monitor. An example of a manufacturer advertising a software product that will monitor employee productivity is FlexiServer (n.d.); currently there are hundreds of attendance and computer use tracking tools.

A survey by the American Management Association in 2007, already old in technology terms, found that the majority of employers in the private sector monitor computer use by their employees, with two-thirds monitoring employees' website visits and blocking connections to websites such as games, 'adult' sites, and so on. Half of the employers tracked the time an employee spent at the keyboard, and an increasing number are monitoring blogs and social networking sites to see what employees are saying about the employer. Nearly half (43%) of companies monitored e-mail, and the capability for technical monitoring has greatly increased in the years since this survey was taken (AMA and ePolicy Institute Research, 2007).

A 2014 survey of 1007 UK employees from companies with up to 1000 staff members found that '75% of respondents use their work-provided computer for non-work activities'. Employers of 40% of those surveyed 'had suffered a major IT disruption caused by staff visiting questionable and other non-work related websites with work-issued hardware, resulting in malware infection and other related issues'. And 10% of the companies 'have lost data and/or intellectual property as a result of the disruption caused by the outage'. Perhaps more surprising, 35% of employees 'would not hesitate to take company property including e-mail archives, confidential documents and other valuable intellectual property from their work-owned computer . . . if they were to leave their company' (Help Net Security, 2014).

People are even more likely to use the same e-mail system for personal and business mail when they work from a home computer. What right does the manager have to see the files on a personal computer, whether at home or at work? In 2013 the information commissioner in the UK published data protection guidance on bringing your own device (BYOD) (Information Commissioner's Office, 2013; Wilson, 2013), in part as a response to a British YouGov survey, which showed that nearly half of British employees use their personal devices for work purposes and 40% do this without guidance from their employers. The information commissioner advised managers to develop a policy on how employees may use their personal devices and to put in place controls to monitor compliance with the policy. In 2015 a US law firm cited four cases related to the use of personal mobile devices in the workplace, pointing not only to lost data but also the difficulties that occur when a company is covered by a litigation hold: 'BYOD complicates the-discovery process because electronic data that may fall within the scope of discovery requests can reside on devices besides those over which the company has control' (Labor Dish, 2015).

Monitoring employees routinely is different from surveying computer usage when a problem arises. In 2013 Harvard University reviewed the work e-mail accounts of 16 residential deans to try to determine who leaked information to the press about an undergraduate cheating scandal at the school. Although the deans were shocked at the search, the employer argued it had a business reason to search them (Hill, 2013).

Would archival managers use such electronic monitoring tools? If there is a concern about employee behaviour they would, and archival management has other tools related specifically to archival work, too. Think about cameras installed in a research room to monitor the behaviour of researchers and provide security for holdings. The cameras do that, but they also show the behaviour of the staff members when in the room. How the camera recordings are handled is a matter for the institution's policy, but it is part of the digital footprints that make up today's documentation. And if the archives have vehicles, GPS (global positioning system) devices may be monitored to see where a vehicle is driven, whether to pick up a donation of personal papers or to go shopping (Privacy Rights Clearinghouse, 2013).

The first indication that flexiplace may not be the only wave in the future sea of work came from the internet corporation Yahoo!. On 22 February 2013, Yahoo!'s chief executive officer, Marissa Mayer, announced the end of flexiplace. The memo to employees said:

> To become the absolute best place to work, communication and
> collaboration will be important, so we need to be working side-by-side.
> That is why it is critical that we are all present in our offices. Some of the
> best decisions and insights come from hallway and cafeteria discussions,
> meeting new people, and impromptu team meetings. Speed and quality
> are often scarified when we work from home. We need to be one Yahoo!,
> and that starts with physically being together.   (Swisher, 2013)

How did Marissa Mayer make that decision? By monitoring the use of Yahoo's virtual private network (VPN). She used the records of employees logging into the network as evidence of remote-worker productivity, which she decided showed that Yahoo! was not getting enough worker engagement and productivity from people who were telecommuting. A leading technology magazine, commenting on the

Yahoo decision, suggested that employers need to set clear rules about requiring employees to use the VPN consistently and to monitor the VPN logs regularly (Samson, 2013).

If employees are permitted to work at a distance, how will their productivity be monitored, if not by electronic means? Clearly, good management of remote employees requires clear productivity measures so both employer and employee know when a product is to be completed and what quality is expected. This requires a more detailed level of project supervision than many archival managers used in the era when management by walking around the office was common.

The nature of the archival workforce

The workforce itself is being reshaped by the easy availability of electronic systems. There are few secretaries today, and staff members who once would have tossed 'filing' into an 'outbox' are now expected to file their own records electronically. Instead of a clerical staff, archives now have computer specialists of all kinds, or the archives contracts for computer services. Social media managers, 'web front-end developers' and 'wikipedians in residence' are now members of the archives staff or its parent organisation.

As noted above, appraisal and description and some reference services are tasks that are susceptible to off-site work if all relevant records are digital. But what of person-to-person reference service, the central feature of the archival research room experience?

This is the area where change is great, whether one looks at the academic research population, the genealogical research users or the general public.

The conversation of academic users with archivist staff, usually by e-mail or text, goes something like this: 'I am a researcher. I want to look at the records of the planning department in country X from the 1970s. What? They're not online? I'll change my research topic!' But even if academic researchers come to the archives, digital equipment has changed the nature of the visit. A study released in December 2012 on the changing research practices of historians pointed out the dramatic change that has taken place since scholars have begun using digital cameras: 'The introduction of digital cameras to archival research is altering interactions with materials and dislocating the process of analysis' with research visits becoming 'more photographic and less analytical.' This, the study suggests, makes 'high-quality finding aids' crucial 'as researchers continue to see their visits to the archive as increasingly photographic and less serendipitous in character' (Ithaka S+R, 2013). Furthermore, in the USA online university courses delivered by star professors from remote locations are rapidly gaining students, and course work graded by anonymous graders or even by computer review is becoming common. How this will shape the future university community is unknown, but it could result in fewer teaching posts and fewer historians to do research in archives. For trends in use of massive open online courses (MOOCs) in historical research see McNeill (2013) and Sumell (2013).

Genealogists too are staying away from archives – in droves. In the USA, genealogists used to account for the overwhelming majority of researcher visits to the archives in a year (one visit per person per day equals one research visit; if a person visits two days in a week, that would be counted as two research visits). Since 2000, as more and more genealogical source materials were digitised and placed online, fewer and fewer people visit archives. For example, in fiscal year 2002 the US National Archives, excluding the presidential library archives, had 241,490 research visits, of which roughly two-thirds (173,783) were researchers using microfilmed records; these were primarily genealogists (NARA, 2002). In fiscal year 2012, the National Archives reported only 20,000 daily visits to use microfilm (NARA, 2012). By 2016 the National Archives did not bother to report the use of microfilm, and the researcher visits nationwide were down to 73,124. An archivist at the National Archive told me that she tries to convince genealogists to visit the archives, arguing that there are many resources that are not online, but to no avail. Researchers use what is online and mostly stop there.

These trends suggest that the research population in archives, at least in the USA, now resembles the research populations of the pre-World War 1 era – before the enormous genealogy boom of the mid-20th century – when academics and users who needed records for legal and rights-related purposes populated the research rooms. The number of reference service staff has decreased because of this decline in on-site users, although the complexity of digital services, explored in more detail by Pierluigi Feliciati in Chapter 6, requires staff with skills in identifying and catering to new user needs and expectations.

If genealogists are not coming and academics – particularly historians – are not staying long enough to read records, where are people using archives? To cite the US National Archives again, its website had over 18 million visits in fiscal year 2012, and its 22 'external blogs and Tumblogs' and 18 'social media toolbox tools' from blogs to Hootsuite had 22 million 'reaches'. And beyond those 40 million hits, according to a National Archives official, the views of National Archives records in Wikipedia articles 'blows all of those numbers out of the water' (see Fretwell, 2013). By 2016 the 'online visits' reached 84 million, or more than twice what it had been just four years earlier.

A survey of the use of social media within archives and manuscript repositories in the USA in July 2012 found that of the 185 respondents, 63% used social media, and nearly half of those not currently using it planned to do so in the future. The majority of the respondents – 51% – worked in archives with only one or two full-time staff members, so engagement with social media is now ubiquitous in the profession (Hopman, 2012). The use of social media in archives is explored further by OCLC Research (Washburn, Eckert and Proffitt (2013) and Bountouri and Giannakopoulos (2014). While these various studies followed different protocols, which do not necessarily allow for easy comparison, in the future archivists – in particular those that use standardised statistical metrics – will be able to compare practices by using a standard of the Society of American Archivists (SAA-ACRL and RBMS, 2018), which counts social media as part of online presence metrics.

Like a number of other repositories, the US National Archives enthusiastically embraces crowd-sourcing techniques, such as asking the public to transcribe handwritten documents that are posted, translate documents in foreign languages into English, and add identifying tags (description) to digitised photographs (for further insights into these participatory approaches see Chapter 9 of this collection). The Archives' staff members select which items will be posted for this public engagement, scan and post them, and manage the process of validating the public work. The validation, like the crowd's work, can be done off-site digitally and does not require a professional archivist.

The ability to perform a task off-site encourages employers to hire contract workers, engaged for specific projects, rather than full-time staff members; limitations of language and perhaps national laws may slow the use of foreign contractors, but not domestic ones. This, too, like the decline in research room visitors, changes the general composition of the workforce.

The emergence of companies that offer full archival services for a fee may encourage smaller institutions to contract for the entire suite of archival functions rather than have an in-house archives staffed by employees. While these companies do not necessarily depend on digital services, they have the ability to work off-site and yet deliver electronically any service or item requested by the contracting institution. Their acceptance as a viable alternative to an in-house archives would surely be less were it not for the digital environment.

Another employment trend is visible, even though it has not entirely penetrated archives. Robots are now used extensively in warehouses, including tape libraries that store computer tapes and other packaged materials. As central archival storage is filled and the cost of building additions becomes prohibitive, particularly in crowded urban areas, off-site storage is the usual solution. And there, in a warehouse setting, robots could retrieve the records and bring them either to a loading area for packing and shipping to the central location or to a station where the items are scanned and sent electronically to the requester and then returned to storage. With the costs of robots falling and as items like the robotic vacuum cleaner begin to show up in offices, the acceptance and use of robots for tasks in archival storage areas will surely come (Young, 2013). And then the work of retrieving and re-shelving performed by the lowest paid staff members will disappear, along with the staff members.

The characteristics of archival leaders

Finally, what impact does the digital environment have on the people who lead archives?

This is perhaps the area where there has been the most fundamental change of all. With very few exceptions, archives are a subordinate unit in an institutional hierarchy. While in the past the heads of major archives, even national archives, usually were professional archivists, increasingly these posts are going to managers and technocrats who do not know the professional techniques employed in the archivists but understand social media, fund raising, and the economic and efficient operation of institutions. Jeffrey Selingo (2008) observed that US university presidents spend most of their time on fund raising, budgeting, community relations and planning; a key leadership trait is their ability to deal with substantial change in organisations; nearly a third have never been faculty members themselves. This is similar to the profiles of the current generation of heads of major archives. We are living in a period of profound change in the world of archives and the world of the academy.

How is the digital climate driving this change? First, archives need to cope with the apparently insatiable public demand for images on the internet. Archives generally do not have the budget to meet the clamour for more images and electronic access, so managers turn to other sources for funds. Mammoth projects have been funded by donors who want to see certain bodies of records digitised. Other bodies of records have been digitised contractually, in which both the archives and the digitising company get copies. In one controversial move, the US National Archives allowed Ancestry, a commercial company, to digitise and place the digital images exclusively on Ancestry's pay-to-view website for five years (researchers could use the images in one of the National Archives' reading rooms but not on the National Archives' own free website (US National Archives and Records Administration, 2008). Library and Archives Canada entered into a similar agreement with an Ancestry subsidiary; when those records will be freely online has not been made public (Gregory, 2013). This adds an access restriction not tied to the nature of material as explored by Gillian Oliver in Chapter 8, but by the digitisation arrangement.

This urgent need for funds to digitise and support electronic records requires archives' leaders to focus on their relationships with resource allocators. Inside the organisational hierarchy the people who control funds, from legislators for government archives to senior vice presidents in private sector organisations, want to see numbers of users an archive has, which now involves counting electronic hits. And they need to hear from happy users. External sources, whether donors or grant-giving organisations, must be persuaded that the archives is worth supporting and really does serve its clientele, and that, too, requires usage numbers and a positive, distinct public image of the archives. This in turn makes archival leaders very sensitive to 'branding' the archives to ensure that the best possible image is put before the funders.

Along with this push to find resources, another major task that has evolved in the digital environment is the need to ensure that there is effective oversight on contracting, now a default way of life in archives. Some contracts are large; for example, to preserve electronic records, build electronic storage facilities for them, and develop electronic workflow systems. The US National Archives announced in November 2012 the award of a contract 'worth up to $7.2 million to oversee the transition of the agency's 4,500 users to the cloud-based Google Apps for email and collaboration' (Howard, 2012).

At the other end of the contracting world are the dozens of contracts with individuals to perform specific services, from transcribers of oral history interviews to exhibit designers. These individual contracts proliferate in part because they usually do not pay benefits (health care, pension contributions) and so are significantly cheaper for the archives than paying full-time staff members to do the same work. Archives have contracted certain services for many years, but the scale of today's contracting – and the need to manage it efficiently – is new and directly related to the digital environment.

This tight trio – fulfilling the demand for immediate access, finding funds to do so, and overseeing contracts – squeezes out the time for almost everything else in a leader's day. Large institutions have long been led by a pair of persons, one focusing on the outside and one focusing on the inside, but today the external demands on directors of archives increasingly isolates them from the internal operations. Does that matter?

It does, in at least three ways. First of all, persuading records creators to turn their records over to an archives, particularly those hard line organisations such as military units or investigative bodies, requires the prestige of the chief archivist. Similarly, in the inevitable disagreements between the archives and records creators over access to records, only the clout of the head of the archives can stand up to the representations of the creating unit. So there are times when only the head of the archives will do, and the leader has to be open and aware of these issues and intervene when needed. If these needs conflict with a fundraising event and the latter wins, in the long run the public loses.

Second, the sheer pressure of the public appetite for digital images causes the leadership to measure success in hits and bits. That is fine, and those access statistics bring in numbers that the archives can sell to funders, but to have images organised in a manner that is intelligible and usable for the general public and the academic user alike requires good arrangement, description and access review. Pressures for more images more quickly can force staff to short change these vital functions, and in the long run the usability of records is undermined.

Third, the focus on the use of digital images by the general public now makes academic users of the archives almost invisible. As reference staff are drained away and description focuses on item description for the public, the academic user's needs are on the way to being ignored. Archivists understand the multiplier effect of the use of archives by academics – they write books whose theories and findings go into textbooks for children and educate the future generations – and they know that many of the records of importance to academic users will not be digitised for many years. If the mono-focus on digitising eviscerates description and reference staff, this will create a situation in which academic users are not given the tools and archival support to do their research. In the long run society will suffer.

As long as archival leaders who are new to archives respect and employ archivists for the professional posts and support them in their decision making, this arrangement can work (see the innovative work on measuring the reciprocal respect between leaders and led by the Respect Research Group, n.d.). After all, hospitals were once run by doctors, but now are run by professional managers. And there is no need for a professional certification in archives to manage staff members who digitise an item, check the transcription of a handwritten letter or push Twitter feeds about new acquisitions or public programmes. But there is a need for archival leaders who recognise that professional archivists have specialised knowledge, professional ethics and a clear sense of service to all who need it.

And as for management by walking around? There's just one word for it in the digital environment: QUAINT.

References

AMA and ePolicy Institute Research (2007) *Electronic Monitoring and Surveillance Survey*, www.plattgroupllc.com/jun08/2007ElectronicMonitoringSurveillanceSurvey.pdf.

American Historical Association (2011) *Telephone and Video Interviews for Academic Hiring: some guidelines*, www.historians.org/Perspectives/issues/2011/1103/1103pro1.cfm.

Beesley, C. (2016) Email, Phone and Social Media Monitoring in the Workplace: know your rights as an employer, blog, US Small Business Administration, www.sba.gov/community/blogs/email-phone-and-social-media-monitoring-workplace-%E2%80%93-know-your-rights-employer.

Bountouri, L. and Giannakopoulos, G. (2014) The Use of Social Media in Archives, *Procedia – Social and Behavioral Sciences*, **147**, 510–17, http://dx.doi.org/10.1016/j.sbspro.2014.07.146.

FlexiServer (n.d.) FlexiServer Productivity and Attendance Software, www.nchsoftware.com/flexi/index.html.

Fretwell, L. (2013) Innovation is Prologue for National Archives' Future, FedScoop, 1 February, http://fedscoop.com/innovation-is-prologue-for-national-archives-future/.

Gregory, R. (2013) Library and Archives Canada Deal with Ancestry.ca Leaves Personal Information Vulnerable, Straight, 7 March, www.straight.com/news/359091/library-and-archives-canada-deal-ancestryca-leaves-personal-information-vulnerable.

Help Net Security (2014) Using Company Devices for Personal Activities Leads to Data Loss, 21 November, www.helpnetsecurity.com/2014/11/21/using-company-devices-for-personal-activities-leads-to-data-loss.

Hill, K. (2013) Harvard Leak Investigation Reminds World that Work Email isn't Very Private, Forbes, www.forbes.com/sites/kashmirhill/2013/03/11/harvard-leak-investigation-reminds-world-that-work-email-isnt-very-private/.

Hopman, R. (2012) Social Media Use in Archives and Special Collections: 2012 results, http://rebeccahopman.com/index/wp-content/uploads/2014/09/2012surveyresults.pdf.

Howard, K. (2012) National Archives Awards Unisys $7.2M Contract for Cloud Email, Federal News Radio, 29 November, www.federalnewsradio.com/240/3137144/National-Archives-awards-

Unisys-72M-contract-for-cloud-email.

Information Commissioner's Office (2013) Bring Your Own Device (BYOD), www.ico.org.uk/for_organisations/data_protection/topic_guides/online/ ~/media/documents/library/Data_Protection/Practical_application/ ico_bring_your_own_device_byod_guidance.ashx.

Ithaka S+R (2013) Supporting the Changing Research Practices of Historians, www.sr.ithaka.org/research-publications/supporting-changing-research-practices-historians.

Labor Dish (2015) What Recent Case Law Can Teach About BYOD Workplaces, www.labordish.com/2015/03/what-recent-case-law-can-teach-about-byod-workplaces.

McNeill, J. (2013) MOOCs and Historical Research, *Perspectives on History*, March, www.historians.org/Perspectives/issues/2013/1303/MOOCs-and-Historical-Research.cfm.

NARA (2002) Measuring Success: performance, in *NARA, Archives Annual Report 2002*, National Archives and Records Administration, www.archives.gov/about/plans-reports/performance-accountability/ annual/2002/2002-annual-report-measuring-success.pdf.

NARA (2012) Measuring and Reporting Our Performance, in *NARA, Performance and Accountability Report*, FY 2012, National Archives and Records Administration, www.archives.gov/about/plans-reports/ performance-accountability/2012/par2.pdf.

Privacy Rights Clearinghouse (2013) Workplace Privacy and Employee Monitoring, fact sheet 7, www.privacyrights.org/fs/fs7-work.htm.

Quast, L. (2012) Social Media, Passwords, and the Hiring Process: privacy and other legal rights, www.forbes.com/sites/lisaquast/2012/05/28/ social-media-passwords-and-the-hiring-process-privacy-and-other-legal-rights/.

Respect Research Group (n.d.) *Scale 'Respectful Leadership'*, University of Hamburg and the Kuehne Logistics University, www.respectresearchgroup.org/scale-respectful-leadership/?lang=en.

SAA-ACRL and RBMS (2018) *Standardized Statistical Measures and Metrics for Public Services in Archival Repositories and Special Collections Libraries*, SAA-ACRL/RBMS Joint Task Force on the Development of Standardized Statistical Measures for Public Services in Archival Repositories and Special Collections Libraries, www.ala.org/acrl/sites/ala.org.acrl/files/content/standards/ statmeasures2018.pdf.

Samson, T. (2013) Can a VPN Log Really Point to Employee Slacking?, *InfoWorld*, 5 March, www.infoworld.com/t/network-monitoring/can-vpn-log-really-point-employee-slacking-213926.

Selingo, J. (2008) As Colleges Evolve, So Must Their Presidents, *Chronicle of Higher Education*, http://chronicle.com/article/As-Colleges-Evolve-So-Must/137635/.

Sumell, A. J. (2013) I Don't Want to be Mooc'd, *Chronicle of Higher Education*, http://chronicle.com/article/I-Dont-Want-to-Be-Moocd/138013/.

Swisher, K. (2013) 'Physically Together': here's the internal Yahoo no-work-from-home memo for remote workers and maybe more, 22 February, http://allthingsd.com/20130222/physically-together-heres-the-internal-yahoo-no-work-from-home-memo-which-extends-beyond-remote-workers/.

US National Archives and Records Administration (2008) The Generations Network Digitization Agreement, www.archives.gov/digitization/pdf/tgn-agreement.pdf.

Washburn, B., Eckert, E. and Proffitt, M. (2013) *Social Media and Archives: a survey of archive users*, OCLC Research, www.oclc.org/content/dam/research/publications/library/2013/2013-06.pdf.

Wilson, E. (2013) Bring Your Own Device? Still the company's responsibility, *The Guardian*, www.guardian.co.uk/media-network/media-network-blog/2013/mar/19/bring-your-own-device-byod-data-risk-security.

World Bank (2013) World Bank Monthly Operational Summary, Africa Region, August, https://tinyurl.com/yd3tnljb.

Young, J. R. (2013) Industrial Revolution: a coming wave of robots could redefine our jobs, *Chronicle of Higher Education*, 29 March, http://chronicle.com/article/The-New-Industrial-Revolution/138015/.

3

The political economy of digital cultural preservation

Guy Pessach

Introduction

Digitisation and distributed communication platforms are responsible for radical transformations in the social conditions of historical truthfulness, social and collective memory institutions, cultural preservation and cultural retrieval practices, as well as many other fundamental changes. For example, one can hardly compare traditional collections of authentic art works, exhibitions and hard copy catalogues with digital images collections of non-profit initiatives such as Artstor Digital Library (www.artstor.org/), commercial images agencies such as Getty Images (www.gettyimages.com/ creative-images) and online photo management and sharing applications such as Flickr.com (www.flickr.com/).

Similarly, one cannot compare traditional celluloid and video archives of television stations with online archives of public broadcasters,[1] video-web-sharing sites such as YouTube.com (www.youtube.com/), content that is available through social networking sites such as Facebook.com and MySpace.com, and personal archiving through peer-to-peer file-sharing networks.[2] Google's Library Project has hardly any resemblance with New York's central public library.[3] The Internet Archive (www.archive.org/)[4] reflects and constructs social memories and (documented) fragments of the past that are notably different from those of the History Channel (www.history.com/), a famous television station offering programming on historical events and people. And – overall – wars, disasters, political events, public affairs, popular culture, high culture, personal items and many other fractions of people's experiences, encounters and lives seem utterly different when they are narrated, contextualised, documented, filtered, preserved and then made accessible via the web.

These are not merely changes in the scope, scale, diversity and attributes of the institutions that are now taking an active role in cultural preservation activities. These are also transformations in the political economy of historical truthfulness – the allocation of resources and powers, economic, technological and legal, which are responsible for shaping landscapes of history and reflections of the past.

Artstor Digital Library is a non-profit initiative, originally founded by the Andrew W. Mellon Foundation, with a mission to create and provide digital images and related materials for scholarly and educational use. Artstor's digital images collection includes over 500,000 images (artefacts) of original art works (most of them tangible) and it is based on partnerships of royalty-free non-exclusive licences with major museums and other cultural institutions (most of them are also subscribers of Artstor).

Getty Images is a commercial agency that collects, digitises and then licenses – for both professional-commercial and private uses – photographs, visual images and stills from audiovisual works.

Flickr is a popular online platform for managing and sharing photographic images.

The BBC digital archive *Treasure Hunt* and the *Creative Archive Licence Group*, piloted in 2005–2006 the Creative Archive Licence which is currently used by the British Film Institute (BFI) and the Open University. (www.bbc.co.uk/creativearchive/).

This chapter argues that the developments taking place in cultural preservation activities are even more radical than we already tend to think they are.[5] Digitised cultural preservation operates in a manner that is very much the reverse of traditional cultural preservation practices. Instead of preservation through governance and control over authentic (original) tangible cultural objects, digitised cultural preservation operates mostly through distribution, diffusion, dis-intermediation and decentralisation of cultural retrieval processes and digitised cultural artefacts. Take for example the case of the recon-struction of the Dead Sea Scrolls. With regard to the reconstructed scroll's original authentic fragments, control over the tangible physical scroll seems essential to secure its continued (physical) existence. Yet, with regard to digital artefacts of the reconstructed scroll, it is distribution and circulation of copies of the reconstructed scroll that would best serve its long-term preservation so it can be made available to the public as a work of cultural significance. (In the extraordinary case *Shanks* v. *Qimron* [2001], the question at stake was the copyrightability of a scholarly work that reconstructed the text of one of the Dead Sea Scrolls by deciphering fragments of the scroll and reconstructing parts missing from it.)

In addition, digitisation shifts cultural preservation from a relatively static model to schemes that are much more dynamic in their intensity, the materials being documented and preserved, and the diversified range of participants – commercial and civic-engaged – now taking part in cultural retrieval and preservation practices. Networked communication platforms tend to generate a regime complex of knowledge intermediaries that destabilise the foundations of conventional and long-established institutions – public-oriented and market-based – of cultural preservation and cultural retrieval. On top of conventional and customary cultural preservation activities by museums, libraries, archives and to a moderate extent also corporate media, we are now entering into an era in which cultural preservation converges and merges with broader circles of content production.

Examples include video web-sharing sites such as YouTube.com, photo-management-sharing sites such as Flickr.com, online music stores, search engines,[6] online databases and peer-to-peer file-sharing platforms. Such frameworks might not target cultural preservation as their main area of activity. Yet, digitised archiving and content retrieval are integral elements and embodied by-products within such schemes. Moreover, information flow itself is also an emerging form of digitised cultural preservation. Peer-to-peer infrastructures are a paradigmatic example of how cultural artefacts and informational works are constantly being stored (preserved), duplicated and then made accessible through numerous accumulative end-points that keep informing on the content that is available through them.

In digital domains, therefore, cultural preservation comprises more than deliberate discretional decision-making processes on the preservation of specific-targeted cultural works. Digitised cultural preservation mashes, converges and integrates with commercial, private and civic frameworks for cultural production and cultural exchange. My purpose in this chapter is to demonstrate the prospects, failures and challenges that this new reality imposes. In particular, I am interested in how the same scale, scope and capacity attributes that empower individual-based cultural retrieval activities are concurrently also forces that make platforms such as YouTube.com or Flickr.com so attractive for corporate media, and therefore, the dialectic tension between social and corporate (commercial) regimes of cultural retrieval and history formation. As Lior Strahilevitz rightfully observed, where there is excess capacity, there is also profit opportunity and consequently the rapid acquisition of social cultural retrieval frameworks by corporate media (a manoeuvre which is then followed by the commercialisation of such networks) (Balkin 2004; Strahilevitz, 2007).

The political economy of the future's past

Cultural preservation – a paradigm shift – from control to distribution

A good starting point for our discussion might be two canonical texts that were written long before the emergence of networked communication platforms: Andre Malraux's *Museum without Walls* (1978) and Walter Benjamin's *The Work of Art in the Age of Mechanical Reproduction* (Benjamin, 1969). Benjamin argued that in the face of photographic reproduction, the original artwork can no longer retain the special value and authority it traditionally possessed (its 'aura'). Two decades later, Malraux took a somehow opposite direction while writing *Museum without Walls* and the fact that in the age of reproduction, the ready availability of cultural artefacts in a variety of contexts, styles and mediums far overreaches the limited revelation of (tangible) art that museums can offer within their (physical) walls.[7] Both Benjamin and Malraux virtually envisioned the key transformation that digitisation would impose – several decades later – on cultural preservation: the transformation from a model of preservation through control and the safeguarding of authentic (tangible) cultural works to a model of preservation through distribution, diffusion and re-contextualisation of (digital) artefacts (reproductions) of cultural works (see Foster, 2002). This last proposition requires some elaboration:

Until recently, cultural preservation had been shaped mostly by paradigms of control over original authentic (tangible) cultural objects. To begin with, the law of cultural property focuses on legal regimes that regulate the use, transfer, preservation and ownership of works of cultural significance (see Fechner, 1998; Gerstenblith, 1995; Merryman, 1989; Merryman and Elsen, 2002). In some circumstances, the law may provide that certain categories of cultural property, such as archaeological objects unearthed by private individuals, are property of the state (see Borodkin, 1995; Merryman and Elsen, 2002, 89, 95–96; Prott and O'Keefe, 1984).

In other circumstances, works of cultural significance that are privately owned may be subjected to legal regimes that impose restrictions on their transferability and manners of use (see for example, Wilkes, 2001). In addition, both market mechanisms and not-for-profit patrons of cultural heritage tend to focus on obtaining ownership and control over authentic cultural objects. Private collectors, dealers and galleries value and price highly the obtaining of proprietary ownership over original authentic cultural objects (an element which then becomes their main source of incentive for further investing in preserving these objects). See Benhamou-Huet (2001) on surveying and describing the dynamics of escalating prices in art markets. Likewise, museums and other types of (non-profit) cultural institutions tend to focus their efforts and resources on obtaining possession, ownership and control over original cultural objects. After all, authenticity and scarcity are the two factors in which much of the value of past cultural works is placed, and with them comes also the inclination towards regimes of proprietary control, as a form of regulating cultural preservation through either market settings or governmental schemes.[8] *The Tragedy of the Commons* (Hardin, 1968), the theory which explains how in shared good contexts individuals could act detrimentally to the common good following their own interests, as well as the Demsetzian argument for property rights – see Demsetz (1967) and Barzel (1989) – seem to apply effectively in the context of tangible cultural preservation: exclusive control is a prerequisite for both the prevention of harm and the provision of incentives to invest resources in the preservation of works of cultural significance.

Digital cultural preservation operates in a reverse mode. Preservation of cultural works' digital artefacts is best served through dissemination and distribution. Once transformed into digital intangibles, the element of control, which had been so essential for tangible cultural works, is seemingly becoming obsolete and even an obstacle in accomplishing the goals of preservation. I have already mentioned the example of the reconstruction of the Dead Sea Scrolls. The same logic applies to many other types of cultural works, including works of art, antiques, musical recordings and audiovisual works. Similar observations are apparent in the public's (right of) access to digital artefacts of cultural works. Preservation, to a very large degree, is not an end in itself but rather a means to secure long term public access to society's cultural treasures (Merryman, 1989). In tangible realms, access to cultural works was mostly achieved by regulating ownership and control over authentic cultural works. One example of this inclination might be the regulation of public access to museums' collections, e.g. the famous case of the Barnes collection in which public law has worked to protect the public interest through judicial oversight of the tax-exempt foundation, which Dr Barnes established to protect his collection and promote his theory of art education (Nivala, 2003). Another example is the proposal for legal recognition in a 'right of access' to cultural works. Price (1975–1976) mentions several such proposals, including the proposals to protect the cultural patrimony of the state, to limit the export of art works, and to pay tax on works of art that are not publicly exhibited. In digital domains we are again witnessing a reverse model: access is best served by distribution and diffusion.

The element of (physical) scarcity of digital intangible artefacts is basically dissolved and so is the fear from physical ruin. Access is therefore best served by distributing multiple copies from (and to) different sources rather than through centralised control.[9] Moreover, one main obstacle for long-term preservation of digitised materials is the problem of longevity – retaining the durability of materials that were either 'born digital' or migrated from tangible or analogue forms into digital modes. As Besser (2000) demonstrated, the key challenge in this context is to overcome problems of technological obsolescence and the relatively short life expectancy of digital media. Yet, in this context also, the problem of longevity is solved, at least partially, by distribution and diffusion through many virtual locations that migrate cultural materials to updated digital formats, rather than by centralised governance of such materials.

A related novel aspect of digitisation is that information flow itself is becoming an emerging form of cultural retrieval and preservation. The nature of information networks, and the internet in particular, is such that multiple digital artefacts of cultural works are concurrently relocated, duplicated, situated and contextualised through many sources (inputs and outputs) that refer, document and provide access to (digitised) artefacts of (the same) cultural works. One example of the nature of information flow as a decentralised-distributed form of cultural retrieval is peer-to-peer (file-sharing) networks, which allow direct exchange of content files among users of compatible applications without any central management and control. Peer-to-peer networks connect individual computers instantly, often using connecting nodes via ad hoc connections. Digital files stored on any user's personal computer could be made available to other users for downloading over the internet.[10] Along with many other utilities and advantages that are associated with peer-to-peer communication networks,[11] the flow of information through peer-to-peer infra-structures is also a dynamic form of cultural retrieval and preservation. Cultural artefacts and informational works are constantly being stored (preserved), duplicated and then made accessible through many accumulative end-points that keep informing of the content that is available through them. One important advantage of peer-to-peer networks in the context of cultural retrieval is their stability and ability to reduce the risk that failures in central servers will have irreversible consequences. Another advantage of such networks that was already mentioned is their diffused and decentralised mechanism for retaining the longevity of materials that were either 'born digital' or migrated – by a numerous number of individuals – from tangible or analogue forms into digital modes.

The nature of information flow as a form of cultural retrieval and preservation encompasses more than just peer-to-peer file-sharing platforms, however. It is the basic architecture of the internet that makes information flow itself a form of cultural retrieval. Although there are different degrees of competence and effectiveness that may vary from one scenario to another, overall, interconnectivity makes each and every personal computer of an end-user a potential node for preserving informational works and then making them available to other users. Web 2.0[12] infrastructures and applications take this inclination one step further by generating web-based social software that enables mass participation in content production and information flow. Clusters of individuals use commons-based frameworks to share content and information through social networking sites (e.g. Facebook.com), digital images management and sharing websites (e.g. Flickr.com) and video-sharing websites (e.g. YouTube.com).

Information flow within such frameworks enables diffused exchange and archiving of cultural works by numerous users who serve as proxies for cultural transmission. In addition, users' indexing and selection applications such as 'tags', 'favourites' and 'profiles' enrich the parameters that underlie cultural retrieval practices, while enabling many individuals to be part of classification and selection mechanisms through which digital knowledge is organised and processed. Information flow therefore makes cultural retrieval and preservation modular and multidimensional.[13] Cultural retrieval and preservation are no longer prescribed only through clusters of static institutional organisations. Rather, cultural preservation is becoming both a form and the outcome of ongoing discourses, manifestations and exchanges of information between organisations, groups and individuals.

Preservation of digital artefacts – of 'information' in its broader sense – also covers much more (content) than preservation of tangible authentic cultural objects. This fact seems to blur the boundaries between 'cultural preservation', 'information retrieval', and cultural production and cultural exchange, and thus inspire re-examination of what falls within and outside the field of cultural preservation. Examples like the Internet Archive, YouTube, iTunes and Google's Library Project all demonstrate one central virtue of digital domains: there are no clear-cut boundaries between the creation of cultural artefacts and their preservation – between 'past' and 'present'. The fact that digitised preservation is best served by distribution and diffusion stimulates a reality in which preservation is being merged into people's ongoing cultural engagements – commercial, civic and private – in networked informational and cultural spheres. This in turn lessens the hegemony that traditional fields of cultural preservation previously possessed.

Digital preservation of culture

The above mentioned observations should not be understood as an argument for full dichotomy regarding cultural preservation before and after the emergence of networked communication platforms. Reproductions and copies of cultural works existed and were common long before the internet revolution. The invention of print, photography, sound recordings, motion pictures and subsequently television all represent landmarks in the continuous evolution of communication tools that, among other functions, have also provided novel means for cultural retrieval and preservation. Yet, as Cohen and Rosenzweig (2005) mention, there are seven qualities of digital media and networks that are responsible for the radical prospects of digital preservation: capacity, accessibility, flexibility, diversity, manipulability, interactivity and hypertextuality (or nonlinearity). These attributes, as well as the decreased costs of establishing and maintaining preservation activities, make the transformation in the scale and scope of (digitised) cultural preservation radical enough to signify a novel reverse model of cultural preservation.

In addition, any comparison between digitised cultural preservation and (tangible) cultural preservation requires a comment on the partial transformation from society's dedication and emphasis on preserving original authentic cultural objects to realms that focus on documenting – and then making available to the public – digitised artefacts. Questions arise: are the cultural and social functions (and value) of these activities at all comparable? Can and should we really talk and refer to traditional tangible cultural preservation and digitised cultural preservation at parallel levels? Recall Benjamin's argument that in the face of photographic reproduction, the original artwork can no longer retain the special value and authority it traditionally possessed (its 'aura'). Moreover, overall, traditional cultural preservation is based on premises that signify and mark authenticity as the central element through which values such as truth, certainty and memory, which establish the public interest in cultural properties, are best served (Merryman, 1989, 346–7), whereas such an element does not seem to apply to digital artefacts.

Admittedly, digital artefacts are incomplete substitutes for the authentic, first and original, copy of a cultural work.[14] Yet, several considerations support a concurrent argument that upholds the value of digitised cultural preservation. To begin with, there are relatively minor functions to the original authentic cultural object for most types of cultural works. Audiovisual works, video-clips, recorded music, photographs and most other types of intangible works – in the age of reproduction – focus on the work's intangible content without assigning unique cultural value to the authentic originating copy.[15] But digital infrastructures are essential as well for preserving tangible cultural works such as paintings, sculptures and architectural masterpieces, which do embrace unique value with regard to the original authentic cultural work. In fact in the most recent years the joint digital infrastructures for tangible and intangible heritage are among the key challenges of the research programmes of the European Commission addressing issues of shared use and re-use, curation and preservation (see Horizon, 2017). At least to some degree, digital artefacts of cultural works embody and magnify similar expressive, aesthetic and historical values that have traditionally established the public's interest in cultural preservation of original authentic tangible art works.[16] Although the value of authenticity of cultural works is not accomplished by digitised cultural preservation, there is still a tradeoff whereas other values such as access are better served when humanity's cultural treasures are made accessible to anyone, from anywhere and without geographical limitations.[17]

Finally, one might also raise some queries about the considerable weight that is given to originating authentic tangible cultural works (as opposed to digital artefacts of such works). The mythisising of authentic originating copies – as irreplaceable by further duplications and reproductions – has its own biases and disruptions. It is considerably influenced by economic motives and social relations. Art markets are an economic business that is significantly based on assigning uniqueness and value to a scarce and limited number of authentic tangible cultural works; there is a whole money-making system whose viability rests on the distinction between 'originals' and 'copies' (see Benhamou-Huet, 2001). Yet, once this economic aspect is put aside, at least some of the proclaimed distinction between authentic cultural objects and their digital artefacts seems to get weaker, especially now that technology enables very high resolution reproductions, including three-dimensional ones, which are practically identical to the original cultural work. Similarly, the special artistic value and authority of an authentic artwork (its 'aura') is to a considerable extent a matter of social relations and practices among people and audiences who either encounter exhibitions of authentic cultural works or collect such works.

One can conclude, therefore, that without undermining the continuous unique importance of authentic (tangible) cultural works, digitised artefacts of cultural works also retain considerable value. I will further elaborate on this point and the democratic culture aspects of digitised cultural preservation in the section 'From cultural institutions to individual-based content-sharing activities', below. At this point, it is enough to return to Andre Malraux's and Walter Benjamin's work and recall that even Benjamin implicitly recognised the fact that with the destruction of artwork's 'aura' and its special status, cultural production and cultural exchange would be democratised. Benjamin emphasised the manner in which reproduction stimulates a manoeuvre from artistic creation to (mass) cultural production and cultural exchange. Similar transformations are apparent also in the context of the move from tangible cultural preservation to digitised cultural retrieval, which leads us to our next topic of discussion: neo-commercialised knowledge intermediaries.

From cultural patrons to cultural retrieval markets

This paradigm shift of cultural preservation – from control to distribution – is also the driving force for the emergence of new profit-motivated intermediaries in the fields of knowledge and cultural retrieval – call them neo-commercialised knowledge intermediaries – that challenge the hegemony of conventional and long-established cultural preservation institutions, such as museums, archives, libraries, state-agencies and even private collectors. For a survey and analysis of traditional cultural preservation institutions see Sax (2001) on private collectors, museums and libraries, and Merryman and Elsen (2002), Gerstenblith (2004) and Meyer (1979) for an historical survey.

Examples begin with commercial enterprises that manage digital collections of cultural works such as Corbis (www.corbis.com/ corporate/overview/ overview.asp) or Getty Images (http://creative. gettyimages.com/source/ home/home.aspx) – agencies that collect, digitise and then license – for professional-commercial purposes and private uses – photographs, visual images (including of art works) and stills from audiovisual works. Similarly, digital retailers of cultural and informational works, such as iTunes (for recorded music), also have long term derivative functions regarding documentation, preservation and the provision of access to cultural and informational works. These examples, however, are just the tip of the iceberg when one considers the case of what used to be mere search engines and are now entities with increasing involvement in building and managing digital archives.

Google serves as a paradigmatic example of a neo-commercialised knowledge intermediary that is already a lead contestant in the fields of knowledge management and digitised cultural preservation. To begin with, Google's core search engine's utilities, such as those of indexing, ranking, linking and in particular caching, are by themselves activities that constantly and dynamically document, map, preserve and provide long-term access to society's cultural and informational landscape. In addition, while relying on its massive storage capacity, computing capabilities and financial resources, Google is constantly developing new information utilities that are far more than those of a mere search engine. Initiatives like Google Scholar (http://scholar. google.com/intl/en/scholar/about.html/),[18] Google Video (http://video. google.com/http://video.google.com/),[19] Google Music Trends (www. google.com/trends/music),[20] Google News Archive Search (http:// news.google.com/archivesearch)[21] and most notably Google Books Library Project are all projects that directly focus on documentation, preservation, selection and provision of access to much of society's cultural and knowledgeable resources; all do so on a scale and with a scope that was not feasible until the emergence of the internet. Overall, neo-commercialised intermediaries' involvement in cultural retrieval is complex and multidimensional, with advantages and disruptions.

Prospects

At the outset, neo-commercialised intermediaries are responsible for outstanding proliferation of large scale knowledge retrieval projects that are based, at least partially, on open-access business models (such that do not charge end-users for using information utilities). It is doubtful whether there are other social agents that would be able, or willing, to invest the same huge amount of financial and technological resources in putting up initiatives with similar documentation and preservation spillovers, such as the ones conducted by Google and other neo-commercialised intermediaries.[22] One prominent example in this context is Google's Library Project, whose staff aim to digitise the full texts of humanity's entire book collections. The contribution of such a project to society's intellectual and cultural landscape is immense; especially when taking into account the fact that Google provides full-text free access to (copyrighted) books that have already fallen into the public domain (Google, n.d.). Google thus provides a gateway to the past's history, culture and knowledge on a scale and with a scope, comprehensiveness and quality that were hardly even imagined until this project was initiated.

In addition, neo-commercialised intermediaries are responsible for two other affirmative transformations in the political economy of cultural retrieval and digital archives. First, neo-commercialised inter-mediaries tend to adopt a content-natural and populist approach to the knowledgeable goods and cultural representations that they document and provide access to. Without undermining problems of information overload as a negative externality cause by copyright works (see Pasquale, 2007) and of commercialisation, when put in a long-term historical perspective, this base-ground is significantly more diverse, multidimensional, democratised and 'truthful' than prior approaches to knowledge and cultural retrieval. A second transformation is the shift towards schemes of indexing and selection that are based on decartelised bottom-up mechanisms for assigning relevance. The most prominent example is Google's ranking algorithm, which is inconclusively based on counting how many sites on the web have linked to a particular site that has the search term in it. In the following paragraphs, I will mention some of the biases and disadvantages that characterise such methods. Yet, overall and when compared to traditional (public) cultural preservation institutions, cultural retrieval practices of neo-commercialised intermediaries seem to be more attentive and responsive to people's preferences. Hence, in terms of their influence on the perception of the past in the future society, cultural retrieval practices of this kind might better document and reflect people's true sense of culture in particular times.

Failures and disruptions

The shift towards rapid privatisation and commercialisation of cultural retrieval and preservation activities also bears several failures and disruptions, some of them with much resemblance to failures and disruptions that are familiar in the context of commercialised (corporate) media markets (Baker, 2002). First, as Rebecca Tushnet has clearly reminded us (2006, 1023), neo-commercialised intermediaries like Google are essentially for-profit organisations. Therefore, no matter how benign such intermediaries have been thus far, one cannot undermine the chance that, in the long run, current business models of open access might be replaced with a movement towards enclosure and pay per use models. In fact, web applications such as Google Book Search, Google News Archive Search and Google Music Trends are already based on business models that concentrate on directing users to commercial sites in which the searched content could be bought.

Similarly, privatised-commercialised realms of cultural preservation tend to subordinate the products of such activities to proprietary regimes and consequently to the typical enclosure spillovers that such regimes are likely to generate. Enterprises like Corbis and Getty Images are explicitly based on proprietary regimes, and even inter-mediaries with an open-access hue, like Google, are providing indications of partial enclosure regimes with regard to some of their cultural retrieval products.[23] In fact, neo-commercialised inter-mediaries like Google already secure their data, technologies and software by a regime of technology-based and (legal) proprietary-based protection mechanisms.[24] The resulting outcome in such cases is that the paradigm of digitised cultural preservation is being pushed back into the traditional models of preservation through control. Only now, instead of being dictated by physical conditions, the model of preservation through control is a product of artificial scarcity based on technological, legal and contractual measures.

Neo-commercialised intermediaries' second category of failures is the biases associated with their architectures – profit-motivated and computer-generated – of indexing, selection and ranking. Profit-motivated biases could be either direct (e.g. decisions made by enterprises such as Corbis and Getty Images on which images to preserve and make available to the public), or more subtle and discreet in their nature (e.g. biased results of searching utilities as a consequence of their advertising policy). Computer-generated biases are more complicated because they tend to exist even when the indexing and selection mechanisms are absent of any commercial manipulation. Indexing and selection mechanisms based on seemingly 'objective' parameters, such as aggregation of popular links, also tend to be lacking because their outcomes are likely to be strongly biased by network effects, power distribution laws and dynamics of a 'winner-take-all' market.[25]

As a consequence, such mechanisms of indexing and selection reflect a canon of cultural representations that practically ignores many other voices and alternatives for organising knowledgeable goods (Introna and Nissenbaum, 2000). To this, one must add the fact that in such markets stakes are also high for the evolvement of concentrated information retrieval spheres that are dominated by a cluster of very few neo-commercialised intermediaries (see Elkin-Koren, 2001; Shirky, 2003). The landscape of history is thus constructed, indexed and organised in a manner that might reflect a somehow particular and narrow dimension of people's lives as well as of people's informational and meaning-making engagements in prior times.

From a broader perspective, once moving from basic website search utilities to other frameworks and expressions of cultural retrieval activities, the whole method of selection through ranking might seem awkward. Within a very short period, enterprises like Google have indeed expanded their wingspan of activities from mere searching utilities to a much wider range of cultural retrieval activities. Yet, overall, the governing interface of indexing and selection has remained more or less the same – top-down automated rankings that assign relevance mostly according to parameters such as automated-processed popularity. At this juncture, one could question the desirability of such a drift and the technological bias that it perpetuates with regard to computerised cultural retrieval activities. The underlying values of a robust democratic culture – self-development, informational autonomy, diversity and semiotic democracy – hardly fit into a matrix that begins one's cultural and informational journey according to a governing meme[26] of top-down-ranked 'relevant' sources. There are long-term expressive disadvantages for customising people's access to culture and memories of the past through governing interfaces of 'winner-take-all' algorithms. Just as in other settings of speech-related matters, the strength of neo-commercialised intermediaries in this context is also their weakness: using selection and preference mechanisms that assign relevance according to majority indications may locate cultural retrieval and preservation practices on a base-ground that is more democratic. Yet, alongside, many voices and reflections of the past are bound to be left unrevealed.

Finally, neo-commercialised intermediaries represent new realities in which knowledge retrieval is dominated by firms that undertake it only as one out of many elements in their business activities. For many neo-commercialised intermediaries, cultural retrieval and preservation utilities are means for gaining audience attention, 'eyeballs' and consumers' loyalty, all in manners that would then be used to advance a broader range of economic interests. Neo-commercialised internet intermediaries are less driven – if at all – by virtues similar to the ones that guide individuals and civic-oriented frameworks in producing, documenting and preserving informational works. Otherwise phrased, the legacy and guiding principles of neo-commercialised intermediaries provide no assurance that their efforts and conduct in cultural preservation will indeed keep track of the public interest. Thus, for example, the commitment of neo-commercialised intermediaries for the continuation and comprehensiveness of their cultural retrieval digital archives is far from being assured. Neo-commercialised intermediaries might abort projects that are not profitable or channel their resources to the retrieval and preservation of materials that are likely to sustain long term profitability. Likewise, neo-commercialised intermediaries' commitment to patron confidentiality and privacy concerns seems to be more doubtful than the long-standing commitment to privacy of public libraries (Vaidhyanathan, 2005). These characteristics of neo-commercialised intermediaries become even more disturbing because of the increasing market dynamism in which civic and commons-based peer production frameworks are either bought or otherwise grouped together with commercial media enterprises. I will return to this point after discussing the role of individuals in digitised cultural preservation.

From cultural institutions to individual-based content-sharing activities

At the other extreme, digitisation signifies the emerging role of individuals and civic-engaged activities in the landscaping of history. To begin with, digitisation and cyberspace have originated several novel types of civic-engaged activities in digital archives.[27] Prominent examples include projects like the already mentioned Internet Archive (https://archive.org/index.php),[28] the Gutenberg Project (www. gutenberg.org/)[29] and the Prelinger Archives (https://archive.org/details/prelinger).[30] In addition, in a networked society, individuals are taking a much more active role in the formation and distribution of content and informational works that among other functions are also historical narratives. First generation examples of this transformation include communicative and speech activities such as blogs, podcasts and other types of amateurs' creative and communicative activities.[31] More recently, new advanced web-based technologies, which are commonly classified under the term Web 2.0, have further empowered the capabilities of individuals to engage in the creation of cultural and informational works and then take part in collaborative sharing of their content through commons-based frameworks. These are some prominent examples:

- *Wikipedia.org* – a free web-based non-profit encyclopaedia based on the contribution of internet users who write, edit and update the content of the encyclopaedia
- *YouTube.com* – a video-web-sharing site that is currently one of the fastest-growing websites on the world wide web; in July 2006, YouTube announced that 100 million clips are watched on YouTube every day; an additional 65,000 new videos are uploaded every day while the site has almost 20 million visitors each month (Wikipedia, 2018d)
- *MySpace.com* – a social networking website offering an interactive, user-submitted network of blogs, profiles, groups, photos, MP3s, videos and an internal e-mail system; the profile utility enables users to create their own personal modular web page in MySpace while corresponding with other profiles; each profile contains two standard 'blurbs': 'About Me' and 'Who I'd Like to Meet' sections, and can contain sections about interests as well as a blog with

standard fields for content, emotion and media that support
uploading images and video-clips
- *Flickr.com* (www.flickr.com/about/) – a popular online photo
management and sharing application.[32]

Most of these frameworks do not target cultural preservation, or even
archiving, as their main area of activity. Yet, digitised archiving,
knowledge and cultural retrieval, and preservation are integral
elements within such schemes for production, exchange and sharing
of content. The historical impact of these frameworks tends to operate
on two main tracks. To begin with, these are platforms that individuals
use in order to upload and distribute copies of existing cultural
materials, including those migrated from another medium (e.g.
chapters of old television programmes). Second, these are platforms
that enable individuals to take a much more active role in
documenting cultural and informational materials and adding one's
personal imprint through organisation, reference, adaptation and
contextualisation of such materials.

The outcome is a web of new paths and directions in the landscaping
of history and the construction of social memories. Just search for a
newsworthy entry or any other type of cultural item on YouTube.com
and immediately you will notice the novel frameworks and
mechanisms through which the various layers of life, people's
experiences and (his)story-telling are being documented, narrated,
situated, contextualised and then potentially preserved for future
generations. Equal but different. Wars, disasters, political events,
public affairs, popular culture, personal items and many other
fractions of people's experiences, encounters and lives are being
created, documented, indexed, classified and then made available to
the public.[33]

It would be a mistake to over-romanticise the impact of these new
frameworks on digitised cultural preservation and the landscaping of
history. These are some of the difficulties apparent within such
platforms:

- manipulations in the production of informational artefacts that
claim to be authentic representations which they are not; the tools
of digitisation make manipulations and forgeries much easier to

accomplish and much harder to detect; for examples of famous photo retouching, including before the digital age, see Wikipedia (2018b)

- privacy concerns about the posting, uploading or even just archiving of materials that abridge privacy interests of individuals
- information overload externalities – as in many other internet settings, the proliferation of individual-based content activities makes it harder to locate and select relevant and useful information and cultural artefacts
- the related impact of network effects and power distribution laws – the economics of human behaviour is such that information flows tend to concentrate audience attention of people to a limited number of sources (e.g. websites or blogs), which then creates path-dependence processes that further increase the centrality of these sources (Huberman, 2001; Shirky, 2003; Watts, 2003).

A full discussion on each of these concerns exceeds the scope of this chapter. Yet, it is worth emphasising that such concerns could be mitigated, at least partially, by legal regulation. Thus, for example, concerns of manipulation could be mitigated if copies of the original authentic cultural works are available through the web in a manner that exposes their later manipulation.[34] And information overload externalities could be mitigated by using retrieval mechanisms, such as search engines, that provide glimpses and snapshots from relevant results, as Pasquale (2007) argues. Moreover, even if such failures and disruptions are taken into account, the potential of decentralised and democratised history formation processes in digital domains still seems more promising than the political economy of historical truthfulness in previous decades (see Benkler, 2006).

Another complexity arises when one examines the dialectics between individual-based activities and neo-commercialised intermediaries. Several examples demonstrate the centrality of market dynamism in which civic and commons-based peer production frameworks are being bought by commercial media enterprises and then the subsequent drift of such frameworks into traditional commercial producer–consumer patterns of content provision and cultural transmission. Corporate media and other commercialised intermediaries are constantly using their economic power to acquire emerging individual-based platforms. Some earlier examples include: the acquisition of YouTube.com by Google for $1.65 billion in stock (News from Google, 2006); the acquisition of the social networking site Myspace.com for $580 million by Rupert Murdoch's News Corporation (the parent company of Fox Broadcasting and other media enterprises) (Wikipedia, 2018a); the acquisition of Flickr.com, the popular online photo management and sharing application, by Yahoo!; and the acquisition of Grouper.com, a web-video-sharing site, by Sony Corp. Entertainment Unit for $65 million (Fox News, 2006).

From the perspective of corporate media enterprises, the reasoning behind such manoeuvres is straightforward: holding on to the market-share, audience attention, technological interface and branded popularity of these new emerging cultural intermediaries. The scale, scope and capacity attributes that empower individual-based cultural-retrieval activities are concurrently also forces that make platforms such as YouTube.com or Flickr.com so attractive for corporate media. Therefore, as Lior Strahilevitz (2007) rightfully observed, where there is excess capacity, there is also profit opportunity and consequently the rapid acquisition of social cultural retrieval networks by corporate media.[35]

From a broader perspective, however, one cannot ignore the speech externalities and cultural costs that these manoeuvres tend to impose on society at large. Acquisitions of this kind transform the social and cultural DNA of these emerging cultural intermediaries to an extent that is much closer to traditional commercial-corporate models of content management.[36] The same audience attention and excess capacity that have developed so quickly owing to the vibrant, pioneering and proliferating nature of user-based content-sharing platforms are now being leveraged by corporate media for their traditional commercial purposes ranging from content provision to selling eyeballs to advertisers.

I am not arguing that dynamics of this kind totally nullify the novel attributes of (the now commercialised) social networks for content production. Nor do I wish to undervalue the important role that corporate media has within a democratic culture. I do argue, however, that such dynamics ultimately leave much less effective space for individual-based activities within user-based content-sharing platforms of this kind. This in turn undermines the role of such platforms in democratising and decentralising the landscaping of history and the construction of social memories.

Summary – a regime complex of digital knowledge intermediaries

The paradigm of digitised cultural preservation therefore represents a dynamic, diversified and complex web of knowledge and cultural retrieval intermediaries. Along with traditional – and relatively static – governmental and public-oriented memory institutions,[37] we are witnessing the emergence of both commercialised and individual-based cultural retrieval platforms. There are transformations not only at the institutional level but also in the types and canons of materials that are being documented, archived and preserved for future generations. The new fields of cultural preservation are also much less isolated and marked from society's ongoing and broader activities of cultural production and cultural exchange than in the past. One reason for this change is the economic potential that commercial knowledge intermediaries have identified in integrating knowledge and cultural retrieval products into their business models. A second reason is the emerging role of individuals in networked cultural production and cultural exchange, especially through collaborative content-sharing platforms. Here also the creation, archiving and making available (to the public) of cultural and informational works is becoming an integrated ancillary element within broader frameworks for content production and content exchange. Digitisation, therefore, implies a transformation in the political economy of historical truthfulness: the allocation of incentives, resources and powers to shape the landscapes of history, social memories and historical imaginations. The transformation from preservation through control (over tangible authentic cultural objects) to preservation through information flow is radical. It is a shift that (potentially) distributes, decentralises and democratises the powers to take part in cultural retrieval and preservation processes.

This somehow utopian vision, however, has to be modified taking into account the variety of funding models of retrieval and preservation of digitised cultural content and the growing pressure for finding business models which seek for financial revenue streams (see

Verwayen and Arnoldus, 2012). The involvement of corporate media and commercial entities in the landscaping of history only begins with commercial ventures of knowledge and cultural retrieval (e.g. digital images agencies such as Corbis.com or the Google Book Project). In addition, corporate media and commercial knowledge intermediaries are constantly attaching themselves to individual-based content-sharing and archiving platforms. This in turn generates dialectic dynamism that in the long run tends to undermine the potential of such platforms to empower the role of individuals in the landscaping of history. The tensions between the different models of cultural preservation and cultural retrieval are following regulations. And since digitised cultural preservation deals with intangible artefacts, copyright law has a central role in regulating the political economy of future's past.

Notes

1   See for example, the BBC digital archive Treasure Hunt (http://bbc.adactio.com/cult/treasurehunt/about/about.shtml) and the recent Creative Archive Licence Group, which makes the BBC's and other institutions archive materials available for download under the Creative Archive Licence (www.bbc.co.uk/creativearchive/).

2   See also Tushnet (2006) discussing the iPod digital music player library (and the iTunes Music Store) as mechanisms that partially replace functions of traditional public libraries. While putting aside the issue of copyright infringements, peer-to-peer file-sharing platforms seems to take this analogy one step further in terms of their preservation and access functions.

3   Google's Library Project (www.google.com/googlebooks/library/), which was announced in co-operation with the University of Michigan, Harvard University, Stanford University, the New York Public Library and Oxford University, digitises and makes searchable the contents of millions of books in the libraries' collections, some of which are in the public domain and some of which are still under copyright. Users have free access to the full text of books in the public domain. Google Library digitises the full text unless publishers object to the digitisation of specific works, but searches retrieve only limited samples, so searchers need to find a way to get a copy of the full book on their own. For a

description of Google Library Project, see Tushnet (2006).

4   A non-profit internet library that documents, preserves and provides access to archived web pages of the entire internet at any given date.

5   For the radical prospects of digital preservation see Cohen and Rosenzweig (2005), who list seven qualities of digital media and networks that are responsible for the revolutionary characters of digital preservation: capacity, accessibility, flexibility, diversity, manipulability, interactivity and hypertextuality (or nonlinearity). See also Balkin (2004), who argues that digital technologies alter the social conditions of speech while making possible widespread cultural participation and interactions that previously could not have existed on the same scale. Balkin also emphasises that the digital revolution has drastically lowered the costs of copying and distributing information, made it easier for content to cross cultural and geographical borders, and lowered the costs of transmission, distribution, appropriation and alteration as well as commenting and building on it. For further discussion, see Elkin-Koren (1996) (who emphasises the contribution of digital technologies in building platforms that enable individuals to take part in identity and meaning-making processes), and Zittrain (2006) (who characterises the internet as based on generative technologies that have capacity for leverage across a range of tasks, adaptability to a range of tasks, ease of mastery and accessibility; these attributes increase the ability of users to generate new valuable uses that are easy to distribute and in turn sources for further innovation). See also Benkler (2006) (who uses economic, political and technological analyses to explain how new information technologies make it easier for individuals to collaborate in producing cultural content, knowledge and other information goods).

6   The paradigmatic example is Google, which in a relatively short period has become a lead contestant in knowledge retrieval and digitised cultural preservation. For further discussion, see 'From cultural patrons to cultural retrieval markets', above.

7   It should be added that along with his observation regarding the decline in the 'aura' of the original art work, at least implicitly, Benjamin also acknowledged prospects of democratisation in the fact that in the age of reproduction, copies of art works, as well as other types of content, are now becoming commodities that are traded in (mass) markets.

8   And indeed, when surveying the main elements of cultural property law, one cannot ignore the role of regulation through control over importation, exportation and transfer of cultural properties (see e.g. the survey in Gerstenblith, 2004). In a similar manner, the debate between the nationalist and internationalist approaches to cultural property law also represents a debate between two different approaches to the allocation of control over cultural properties (see Merryman, 1986).

9   I am not ignoring the question whether – and to what extent – intellectual property protection is required in order to provide a threshold of incentives to invest in digitisation of cultural materials and their making available to the public. Yet there are several types of incentives – other than intellectual property protection – that might provide the required framework of incentives in this context.

10 Peer-to-peer architecture takes decentralisation a step further by enabling all users connected to a peer-to-peer network to share resources. In peer-to-peer architecture, users are not only consuming services but are providing resources, such as bandwidth, storage space, computing power and content. In fact, this principle goes back to the origins of the internet as conceived by US Defense Department military strategies, whose aim was to build a computer network that would be resilient to attacks. The theory was that a distributed network would be more resilient than a centralised network to repeated attacks. A packet switching technology was designed to serve this strategic goal, thus reducing dependency on central control systems and securing continuous service even in the case of major damage resulting from nuclear or other strategic attacks. Since then, decentralisation remained the governing principle of internet transmission. The distributed nature of internet communication was facilitated by the use of open protocols, primarily the TCP/IP protocol, which enabled interconnection among independent and incompatible computers and information systems.

11 Among them are the efficiency of peer-to-peer networks in allocating resources for distribution and consumption of informational works, the ability of peer-to-peer networks to enhance personal freedom and diversity through its decentralised architecture and the low cost of making content available through peer-to-peer networks (Elkin-Koren, 2006).

12 The term Web 2.0 refers to second-generation services available on the world wide web that enable people to collaborate and share

information online. In contrast to the first generation internet utilities, Web 2.0 gives users an experience closer to desktop applications than the traditional static web pages. Web 2.0 applications often use a combination of techniques devised in the late 1990s, including public web service application programming interfaces (dating from 1998), and web syndication (1997). They often allow for mass participation – web-based social software – such as wikis – in which clusters of individuals use commons-based frameworks to share content and information (Wikipedia, 2018c).

13 See also Zittrain (2006), who characterises the internet and the personal computer as generative, embodying technologies that have four main attributes: capacity for leverage across a range of tasks, adaptability to a range of tasks, ease of mastery, and accessibility.

14 See also Malraux (1978). A full discussion on this point exceeds the scope and purpose of this chapter, yet one must bear in mind that the unique value assigned to an originating art work is to a very large extent an outcome of social conceptions on the special value, authority and presence of the original copy (as opposed to its artefacts).

15 Indeed, collectors and people in general might assign value to ownership of rare originating copies of intangible goods (such as the original master recording of the Beatles' *Abbey Road*) (see e.g. Stoller, 1984). Yet, this value would be mostly distinct from values that underlie cultural preservation (see note 27). Authenticity might still serve as a best evidence rule for the originating content of the cultural work. I will return to this point while discussing the issue of manipulations in the section 'From cultural institutions to individual-based content-sharing activities', above. Yet, while taking into account this caveat, in many circumstances, most of the values that underlie cultural preservation are served also by copies of intangible works that 'were born intangible'.

16 One should also take into account that similar interests exist also in the context of cultural works that were 'born digital' whereas there is no originating tangible cultural object. Examples include digital art, video games and software.

17 John Henry Merryman, who is regarded by many as the lead theorist of cultural property law, has emphasised the intrinsic expressive value of cultural property as embodying the values of truth, memory and the shared significance of cultural works to communities and individuals

within them. Merryman (1986; 1989) has identified two central elements of cultural property policy: preservation and access.

18 Google Scholar provides search utilities and partial free access to scholarly works across many disciplines and sources: peer-reviewed papers, theses, books, abstracts and articles, from academic publishers, professional societies, preprint repositories, universities and other scholarly organisations.

19 Google Video is defined by Google as 'the first online video market'. It provides search, indexing and access utilities to all types of audiovisual content, and includes both free content and premium content that has to be purchased. It enables users to upload their content and share with other users.

20 Google Music Trends is an application that gathers and analyses the listening habits of end-users according to the music they play in their personal media players. It then builds daily and statistical snapshots of the most popular music, with links to commercial websites in which the music could be bought.

21 Google News Archive Search provides searching utilities in historical news archives. Some content is accessible to all users and some requires a fee.

22 The collections of a number of national libraries had been since digitised in collaboration with Google Books (https://en.wikipedia.org/wiki/Google_Books).

23 As Tushnet (2006) demonstrates, Google has demanded some of the university libraries participating in Google's Library Project to use technological measures that would restrict automated access to libraries' digital copies and to attempt to stop redistribution of those copies, regardless of whether the digitised materials at stake are of works that have already fallen into the public domain.

24 Neo-commercialised intermediaries may use an open-access model as their strategic business model, yet they would still retain control and claim ownership over the pipelines of access to their databases and archives. One example is the interface between Google's various databases of informational works (e.g. those of Google Print or Google Library Project) and the searching or indexing architecture that users are practically compelled to use in order to co-ordinate their access to the contents of such databases. Effective freedom to browse, as well as effective freedom to apply one's own searching and selection

parameters, require 'full access to raw databases' applications that neo-commercialised intermediaries do not tend to adopt, especially in their own unique and exclusive databases. Instead, users are usually required to rely solely on the searching architecture that such intermediaries adopted.

25 Network economy or network effects is the economic circumstances of increasing return to the scale of demand (Katz and Shapiro, 1985, 424). Power law distributions tend to arise in social systems where many people express their preferences among many options. As the number of options rise, people tend to concentrate on a smaller number of options (see generally Huberman, 2001; Watts, 2003).

26 Memes are units of information and culture that replicate and evolve in accordance with principles of competitive selection. Recent literature has shown how memetic dynamism influences our cultural notions and preferences. See Cotter (2005) and Balkin (2003).

27 There are many digital cultural heritage schemes. Examples include the national digital information and infrastructure and preservation programme (www.digitalpreservation.gov/), a project directed by the Library of Congress, which is intended to develop a national strategy and support particular projects to collect, archive and preserve the burgeoning amounts of digital content, especially materials that are created only in digital formats, for current and future generations; Making of America (www.hti.umich.edu/m/moagrp/), which is a joint project of Michigan and Cornell universities, supported by the Andrew W. Mellon Foundation, intended to preserve and make accessible through digital technology a significant body of primary sources related to development of the US infrastructure; JSTOR (www.jstor.org/), Artstor (www.artstor.org/info/) and Aluka (www.aluka.org/?cookieSet=1), three Ithaka projects to create digital libraries of digital images (Artstor), scholarly journal (JSTOR) and scholarly resources from and about the developing works (Aluka); the European Commission's former Digital Libraries Initiative on the digitisation and online accessibility of cultural materials and digital preservation (https://eur-lex.europa.eu/legal-content/EN/TXT/ ?uri=LEGISSUM%3Al24226i); national initiatives for digital cultural preservation such as Sweden Royal Library's Kulturars project (www.kb.se/kw3/ENG/), which is intended to preserve and make accessible everything found on the Swedish internet; or the Australian

National Library Pandora project (http://pandora.nla.gov.au/overview. html), which collects and provides long-term access to selected online publications and websites about Australia, by an Australian author on a subject of relevance to Australia, or by an Australian author of recognised authority that contribute to international knowledge. Such activities in many respects continue the long-standing involvement of governmental and non-profit cultural institutions in cultural heritage and cultural preservation. These initiatives demonstrate that public and non-profit cultural institutions have taken seriously the digital revolution and its prospects in the context of cultural preservation.

28   The Internet Archive is a non-profit digital library offering free universal access to books, movies and music, as well as 423 billion archived web pages, with an attempt to digitise and preserve the entire world wide web at any point of time.

29   The Gutenberg Project volunteer organisation digitises, archives and distributes cultural works – mostly full texts of public domain books – as freely as possible, in long-lasting, open formats that can be used on almost any computer.

30   Founded in 1983 by Rick Prelinger, Prelinger Archives have collected over 48,000 'ephemeral' (advertising, educational, industrial and amateur) films. The archive collects, preserves and facilitates access to films of historic significance that have not been collected elsewhere. Included are films produced by and for many hundreds of important US corporations, non-profit organisations, trade associations, community and interest groups, and educational institutions. The Library of Congress acquired the film collection in 2002, yet Prelinger Archives continues its activity, while its collections (including those that were sold to the Library of Congress) are available for free online public access through the Internet Archive. The Prelinger Archives story exemplifies how civic-engaged activities in documentation and preservation could be good proxies for identifying and focusing on cultural and informational fields that traditional institutions have thus far neglected.

31   See generally Hunter and Lastowka (2004) and Balkin (2004, 7–16) emphasising the rising novel role of individuals as producers and distributors of content. See also Cohen (2005) analysing and describing different models and types of users, including the romantic user, the postmodern user and the situated user, all of which engage and play,

though under various motives and beliefs, in the fields of communicating through creative activities and creating through communication frameworks.

32 Flickr allows photo submitters to categorise images by use of keyword 'tags' (a form of metadata), which allow searchers to find images on a certain topic such as a place name easily. Flickr provides private and public image storage. A user uploading an image can set privacy controls that determine who can view the image. A photo can be flagged as either public or private. Private images are visible by default only to the uploader, but can be marked as viewable by friends and/or family.

33 Thus for example, during the 2006 Israeli-Hisballa-Lebanese war, people from Israel, Lebanon and other Arab countries uploaded a significant number of video-clips on the war and its ricochets, which were either created by those individuals or were adaptations and transformative works that rely on existing (mostly television) materials. Although one should be very cautious about the authenticity of at least some of these materials, they are still invaluable primary sources that will provide future generations with scenes, information, perspectives and reflections on people's views of the war – such that are not fully covered through mainstream mass media institutions. Decentralisation, democratisation and multidimensional visualising in the process of history formation are therefore key elements in the transformation that digitisation embodies.

34 There is a thin line between 'manipulating' informational works and making legitimate use of existing informational works in the course of formatting additional transformative historical narratives that wish to be based on and correspond with existing cultural and informational materials.

35 See also Balkin (2004, 13–15), who emphasises the social contradictions of the digital revolution as producing two conflicting crucial trends: the democratisation of digital content and the increasing importance of digital content as a source of wealth and economic power. According to Balkin, these trends quickly come into conflict because the very same features of the digital age that empower ordinary individuals also lead businesses continually to expand commercial markets for intellectual property and digital content. The approach presented in the main text is even more pessimistic than the one presented by Balkin. It argues

that the main threat for successful emerging civic-engaged frameworks is not only of enforcement – by intellectual property owners – but also of the buying power of corporate media and their intense taking over of successful individual-based platforms. Indeed, intellectual property regimes play a central role in pushing emerging civic-engaged platforms into the hands of corporate media. Yet, much of the transformation in the nature of individual-based activities derives from the dialectic tension between excess capacity and profit opportunity – a tension which rapidly leads to the acquisition of such platforms by corporate media.

36 One example was the plan of record companies and YouTube.com to offer, through YouTube, current and archive music videos clips of record companies. The plan was to offer the videos free of charge and to use advertisements as the main source of revenue (see the report in http://news.bbc.co.uk/2/hi/entertainment/4798133.stm). In addition, YouTube plans on implementing technological tracking mechanisms for identifying the use of copyrighted materials (including within derivative home-made videos that use such materials).

37 Public and not-for-profit initiatives in digital cultural preservation benefit from several important advantages in their ability to manage large scale projects that require considerable financial resources, capacity and co-ordination between cultural institutions around the globe. In many respects, such activities continue the long-standing involvement of governmental and not-for-profit cultural institutions in cultural heritage and cultural preservation. Cultural preservation has the attributes of a public good so it was only natural that it would be provided either directly through state institutions or through not-for-profit cultural institutions. Public and not-for-profit initiatives are also characterised by their stability and commitment for long-term comprehensive preservation projects regardless of profitability considerations. They are generally characterised by a legacy and a strong sense of public–civic responsibility, and a commitment to the value of guaranteeing equal public access to information and cultural works. These attributes demonstrate the important role of public initiatives in the context of digital archiving and cultural preservation. Nevertheless, public and not-for-profit knowledge intermediaries suffer from several disadvantages that signify the bounded role of such institutions within a democratic vision of building digital

infrastructures for cultural retrieval and preservation. Public initiatives for digital cultural preservation tend to represent a relatively static and elitist model. They are usually constrained by a social understanding of culture that concentrates on (digital) preservation of cultural works that have (already) fallen into some 'canonical field' of public, social, national or aesthetic interest and tend to have a centralised element of guidance – some would say patronisation – in building digital cultural collections and in their indexing and selection mechanisms. Hence, as this chapter argues, a democratic culture demands a social-political understanding of cultural heritage and digital history that is significantly more dynamic, open, ample, diversified and populist than the one that is usually offered by public knowledge intermediaries. I by no means intend to undermine the centrality of public digitised cultural preservation activities within the broader framework of digital cultural retrieval. Yet, our discussion suggests that there is more to accomplish in the fields of cultural retrieval and digital landscaping of history.

References

Baker, E. C. (2002) *Media, Markets and Democracy*, Cambridge University Press.

Balkin, J. (2003) *Cultural Software: a theory of ideology*, Yale University Press.

Balkin, J. M. (2004) *Digital Speech and Democratic Culture: a theory of freedom of expression for the information society*, Faculty Scholarship Series, http://digitalcommons.law.yale.edu/fss_papers/240.

Barzel, Y. (1989) *Economic Analysis of Property Rights*, Cambridge University Press.

Benhamou-Huet, J. (2001) *The Worth of Art: pricing the priceless*, Assouline, 36.

Benjamin, W. (1969) *Illuminations: essays and reflections*, edited by Hannah Arendt, translated by Harry Zohn, Schocken Books.

Benkler, Y. (2006) *The Wealth of Networks: how social production transforms markets and freedom*, Yale University Press.

Besser, H. (2000) Digital Longevity, in M. K. Sitts (ed.), *Handbook for Digital Projects: a management tool for preservation and access*, www.nedcc.org/assets/media/documents/dman.pdf.

Borodkin, L. J. (1995) The Economics of Antiquities: looting and a proposed legal alternative, *Columbia Law Review*, **95** (2), 377–417.

Cohen, D. and Rosenzweig, R. (2005) *Digital History: a guide to gathering, preserving, and presenting the past on the web*, University of Pennsylvania Press.

Cohen, J. E. (2005) The Place of User in Copyright Law, *Fordham Law Review*, **74**, 347–74.

Cotter, T. F. (2005) Memes and Copyright, *Tulane Law Review*, **80** (2), 332–47.

Demsetz, H. (1967) Toward a Theory of Property Rights, *American Economic Review*, **57** (2), 347–59.

Elkin-Koren, N. (1996) Cyberlaw and Social Change: a democratic approach to copyright law in cyberspace, *Cardozo Arts & Entertainment Law Journal*, **14** (2), 215–95).

Elkin-Koren, M. (2001) Let the Crawlers Crawl: on virtual gatekeepers and the right to exclude indexing, *Dayton Law Review*, **26** (179), 187–91.

Elkin-Koren, N. (2006) Making Technology Visible: liability of internet service providers for peer-to-peer traffic, *New York University Journal of Legislation and Public Policy*, **9** (16), 19–24.

Fechner, F. G. (1998) The Fundamental Aims of Cultural Property Law, *International Journal of Cultural Property*, **7** (2), 376–94.

Foster, H. (2002) Archives of Modern Art, *The MIT Press Journal*, **99**, (October), 81–95.

Fox News (2006) Sony Pays $65 Million for Web-Video-Sharing Site Grouper.com, 23 August, www.foxnews.com/story/2006/08/23/sony-pays-65-million-for-web-video-sharing-site-groupercom.html.

Gerstenblith, P. (1995) Identity and Cultural Property: the protection of cultural property in the United States, *Boston University Law Review*, **75**, 559.

Gerstenblith, P. (2004) *Art, Cultural Heritage and the Law: cases and materials*, Carolina Academic Press.

Google (n.d.) About Google Books, http://books.google.com/intl/en/googlebooks/about/index.html.

Hardin, G. (1968) The Tragedy of the Commons, *Science*, **162** (3859), 1243–48.

Horizon (2017) Horizon 2020, Work Programme 2018–2020. 13. Europe in a changing world – Inclusive, innovative and reflective societies, http://ec.europa.eu/research/participants/data/ref/h2020/wp/2018-2020/main/ h2020-wp1820-societies_en.pdf.

Huberman, B. A. (2001) *The Laws of the Web: patterns in the ecology of information*, MIT Press.

Hunter, D. and Lastowka, F. G. (2004) Amateur-to-Amateur, *William & Mary Law Review*, **46** (3), 951–1030.

Introna, L. and Nissenbaum, H. (2000) Shaping the Web: why the politics of search engines matters, *The Information Society*, **16** (3), 169–85.

Katz, M. L. and Shapiro, C. (1985) Network Externalities, Competition, and Compatibility, *American Economic Review*, **75** (3), 424–40.

Malraux, A. (1978) *The Voices of Silence*, translated by Stuart Gilbert, Princeton University Press, 12–128.

Merryman, J. H. (1986) Two Ways of Thinking about Cultural Property, *American Journal of International Law*, **80** (4), 831–53.

Merryman, J. H. (1989) The Public Interest in Cultural Property, *California Law Review*, **77** (2), 339–64.

Merryman J. H. and Elsen, A. E. (2002) *Law, Ethics and the Visual Arts*, 4th edn, Kluwer Law International.

Meyer, K. (1979) *The Art Museum: power, money, ethics*, William Morrow.

News from Google (2006) Google to Acquire YouTube for $1.65 Billion in Stock, http://googlepress.blogspot.bg/2006/10/google-to-acquire-youtube-for-165_09.html.

Nivala, J. (2003) Droit Patrimoine: the Barnes Collection, the public interest and protecting our cultural inheritance, *Rutgers Law Review*, **55**, https://ssrn.com/abstract=2176920.

Pasquale, F. (2007) The Law and Economics of Information Overload Externalities, *Vanderbilt Law Review*, **60**, 70–131.

Price, M. E. (1975–76) State Arts Councils: some items for a new agenda, *Hastings Law Journal*, **27**, 1183–1205.

Prott, L. V. and O'Keefe, P. J. (1984) *Law and the Cultural Heritage*, vol. 1, Discovery and Excavation, Professional Books Ltd.

Sax, J. L. (2001) *Playing Darts with a Rembrandt: public and private rights in cultural treasures*, University of Michigan Press.

Shanks v. *Qimron* [2001] C.A. 2811/93, 54(3) P.D.817, English translation in *European Copyright and Design Reports* 2001, 73.

Shirky, C. (2003) *Power Laws, Weblogs and Inequality*, http://shirky.com/writings/powerlaw_weblog.html.

Stoller M. A. (1984) The Economics of Collectible Goods, *Journal of Cultural Economics*, **8** (1), 91–104.

Strahilevitz, L. J. (2007) Wealth Without Markets?, *Yale Law Journal*, **116**, 1472–1516, http://digitalcommons.law.yale.edu/ylj/vol116/iss7/2.

Tushnet, R. (2006) My Library: copyright and the role of institutions in a peer-to-peer world, *UCLA Law Review*, **53** (4), 977–1030.

Vaidhyanathan, S. (2005) A Risky Gamble with Google, *Chronicle of Higher Education* (2 December),
http://chronicle.com/weekly/v52/i15/15b00701.htm.

Verwayen, H. and M. Arnoldus (2012) A Business-model Perspective on End-users and Open Metadata. In M. Dobreva et al. (2012) *User Studies for Digital Libraries Development*, Facet Publishing.

Watts, D. J. (2003) *Six Degrees: The Science of a Connected Age*, W. W. Norton & Company.

Wikipedia (2018a) Myspace, https://en.wikipedia.org/wiki/Myspace.

Wikipedia (2018b) Photo Manipulation,
https://en.wikipedia.org/wiki/Photo_manipulation.

Wikipedia (2018c) Web 2.0, https://en.wikipedia.org/wiki/Web_2.0.

Wikipedia (2018d) YouTube, https://en.wikipedia.org/wiki/YouTube.

Wilkes, N. B. (2001) Public Responsibilities of Private Owners of Cultural Property: toward a national art preservation statute, *Columbia-VLA Journal of Law & the Arts*, **24** (2), 177–212.

Zittrain, J. L. (2006) The Generative Internet, *Harvard Law Review*, **119** (7), 1974–2040.

4

Legal issues surrounding digital archiving
Oleksandr Pastukhov

Background

Archiving is as old as recorded knowledge. As soon as man had more than one clay tablet, papyrus or parchment scroll stored at one place, the archive was born. Over the centuries that followed, a plethora of rules were developed regarding ownership, acquisition, appraisal, arrangement, use, preservation, management and access to the collections of documents we now call 'archives'. Gradually, those rules gained more and more legal character – they were created or sanctioned by the state and enforced by the government.

Governments take interest in archives for many reasons, the most important of which is control: the government wants to know who owns what, how much money in taxes can be collected, what resources can be allocated to particular public policies, and so on. This explains why property, corporate and shareholder registries exist, why taxpayers are obligated to preserve their accounting books, and why government agencies and private companies are required to keep records of their activities.

Individuals and companies are equally interested in retaining documents for future use. In order to turn to the government for protection of their interests, natural and legal persons have to demonstrate that they are entitled to certain legal rights. In most cases, the only way to do that is to produce a document, such as a birth certificate, a driving licence, a diploma, a ticket, a visa, a membership card, a contract, an invoice or a receipt.

Besides the uses of archives to support governmental or business functions, there are currently also archives of historical documents, which are used mostly for research and teaching. These archives expand digital access to their holdings. Such activities also touch on a number of legal issues ranging from the rights invoked by sharing content to specific conditions of access.

In today's world of interconnected computers, storing and examining tangible originals of documents, such as those mentioned above, is no longer necessary in many cases. The same applies to the objects of art, even three-dimensional ones. Preserving and consulting digital representations of those objects is usually enough, so property rights remain relevant only in a limited number of scenarios, when physical access to the artefact is needed. Instead, the digital format of the materials resulting from scanning two- and three-dimensional objects involves other areas of law, primarily copyright and privacy, both of which are the focal points of this chapter.

Copyright

How copyright is involved

The rights of authors and other copyright holders, collectively known as copyright, are invoked by digital archiving primarily for the following two reasons. First, most of the materials being digitised (handwritten documents, printed matter, photographs, image and sound recordings) are works of art in the legal sense and thus potentially form the subject matter of copyright. Second, since the technological processes used for digitisation and communication to the public require multiple copying, the issue of potentially illegal copying under copyright law arises.

Users' behaviour also potentially invokes copyright. Consulting documents stored in a digital archive, saving their contents in computer memory, forwarding them to others – all these actions involve copying of potentially copyrightable materials.

It becomes apparent from the extensive use of the word 'potentially' above that not all of the materials memory institutions deal with are subject to copyright protection. Hence, before considering digitisation, a memory institution should answer the following questions:

- Is the material copyrightable at all?
- Is it in fact copyrighted?
- If so, who holds the copyright?
- What cannot be done with the work without the copyright holder's permission?

Let us start with defining copyright subject matter and investigating the requirements works must meet to be protected by copyright – answering the question 'What is copyrightable?'

What is copyrightable?

In all the countries where copyright exists, it protects a variety of literary, scientific and artistic works. As a rule, national copyright laws and international conventions do not define the works' subject matter of copyright, but contain a non-exhaustive list of typical works of art to which protection is afforded. Usually, such lists include the following categories:

- literary works
- dramatic works
- musical works
- audiovisual works
- pictorial, graphic and sculptural works
- photographs
- architectural works
- maps, charts, plans, etc. (Malta, 2000, Art. 3(1)(a); USA, 1976, §102(a); WIPO, 1979, Art. 2(1)).

It is not the material objects in which works of art are being embodied that enjoy protection, but the works themselves. When selling property rights in the material object that embodies the work of art, its author or other copyright holder does not lose copyright in the work. Correspondingly, the buyer of the object buys nothing more than that – the object – and acquires no rights vested in authors and other copyright holders.

It is also not the underlying ideas or facts described in or by the work of art that are protected by copyright law, but the artistic expression thereof. Accordingly, anyone is free to write their own story about Martians invading the Earth or to cook following recipes described in a cookbook. Ideas are protected by another branch of intellectual property law – patent law.

Accordingly, materials such as news reports, folklore works, transport schedules, tables of scales and measures, as well as state documents, symbols and insignia are usually excluded from the scope of copyright protection (Bulgaria, 1993, Art. 4; USA, 1976, §105). They belong to what is known as the 'public domain' – they can be freely used by everyone. Sheer numbers of such unprotected materials are available at archives, libraries, museums and other memory institutions and most of them communicate mere facts. Copyright law does not extend its protection to facts, as well as 'any ideas, theories, principles, methods, procedures, processes, systems, manners, concepts, or discoveries, even if they have been expressed, described, clarified or illustrated in a work' (Ukraine, 1993, Art. 8(3)). This being said, the copyrightability of bibliographic data (metadata) and linked data remains disputed (Coyle, 2013; Rodríguez-Doncel et al., 2016).

Works resulting from a creative recast of works of all the above mentioned categories are protected as derivative works on equal terms with the works on the basis of which they have been created without prejudice to the rights of the authors of the underlying works (Ukraine, 1993, Art. 8(1)(1); USA, 1976, §103; WIPO, 1979, Art, 2 (3)).

Collections of works of all of the above categories, including derivative works, provided they meet the originality criterion, are subject to copyright protection 'as such without infringing the rights of the authors of each work being part of such collections' (WIPO, 1979, Art. 2(5)). The originality of collections results from the creative work on the selection, co-ordination or arrangement of the materials included into their contents (USA, 1976, §101 (definition of 'compilation'); Ukraine, 1993, Art. 8(1)(1); WIPO, 1979, Art. 2(5)).

One particular type of collective works are databases. These works considerably facilitate the processes of storing, transferring and searching for information by memory institutions. Copyright protects only the selection, co-ordination and arrangement of the materials included in databases consisting of works in the public domain. However, copyright does not prohibit free use of the same materials. Moreover, a great number of databases are not subject to copyright protection at all, since they do not meet the originality criterion despite possibly considerable efforts and investments necessary for their creation. An example of such databases are telephone directories, whose arrangement in the alphabetical order is far from original (*Feist Publications, Inc.* v. *Rural Telephone Service Co.* [1991] 1287). In order to compensate creators of databases and to stimulate their creation, a sui generis protection regime for databases was created in the European Union (EU) in 1996 by means of a special directive, according to which databases are subject to legal protection if their creators have made considerable investments in the obtaining, verification and presentation of their composite elements. Draft bills to the same effect keep being introduced in the US Congress, but to no avail so far.

A more troublesome type of collective works are multimedia works. Those works result from the combination of two or more categories of works in one medium. The most appropriate of all currently available kinds of media for such combination are digital ones. While the existence of copyright protection of multimedia works is undoubted, the scope of this protection cannot be easily defined. The problem is that multimedia works are a result of the process of convergence of various types of works, each with its own scope of protection and guided by a different set of rules.

Is the work in fact copyrighted?

A great number of the above mentioned literary and artistic works can be found at memory institutions and all of them – again, potentially – can be copyright-protected, but belonging to one of the categories of works mentioned in the law is not enough. To be protected under copyright law, a work should meet specific criteria of originality, fixation, formality and duration, addressed in detail below.

Originality

Different countries interpret the first criterion in more or less the same way. The courts in the countries of Anglo-Saxon (common) law interpret the criterion of originality broadly: the work should be simply a result of independent work and talent of the author – not copied from other copyrighted works, and should possess 'at least some minimal degree of creativity' (*Feist Publications, Inc.* v. *Rural Telephone Service Co.* [1991] 1287).

Besides the creativity criterion, courts in the countries of continental (civil) law also consider whether the work bears the mark of the author's personality or reflects their individuality (Berenboom, 2005). Nowadays, however, these requirements are becoming more flexible due to the advent of new kinds of works whose creation is a product of artificial intelligence (Bridy, 2012).

'Originality' in copyright does not imply 'artistic value' and does not presuppose a high aesthetical level of the work or an impeccable artistic taste of their creators. Neither is 'originality' a synonym of 'novelty'. Thus, two identical works, created by different authors, each ignorant of the other, will be copyrightable even if the one created later is not novel.

Fixation

Approaches to the second criterion are not the same in countries of different legal traditions. In the USA, for instance, copyright protection is afforded to materials 'fixed in any tangible medium of expression now known or later developed, from which they can be perceived, reproduced or otherwise communicated either directly or with the aid of a machine or device' (USA, 1976, §102(a)). Moreover, a work is considered 'fixed', if the tangible medium appears to be 'sufficiently permanent or stable to permit it to be reproduced or otherwise communicated for a period of more than transitory duration' (USA, 1976, §101). As a result of this approach, in accordance with the US legislation, oral, drama, musical or choreographic works not fixed on film or any other medium, as well as works broadcasted live without being simultaneously recorded are not considered 'fixed' and are thus not protected by copyright (USA, 1995, 32). Other countries influenced by Anglo-Saxon law, including Malta, normally follow this approach (Malta, 2000, Art. 3(2)).

In the countries of continental Europe, copyright laws require the protected work to be fixed in some form, but not necessarily in a 'material' one. Thus, the Bulgarian Law extends its protection to works expressed in 'whatever objective form' – a form that allows perceiving the works by the humans' perceptive organs (Bulgaria, 1993, Art. 3(1)).

This way, oral, drama and choreographic works meet the established legal requirements for representations in an objective form and are protected by copyright law in Bulgaria regardless of their fixation in a tangible medium.

Formalities

In the states party to the Berne Convention, the protection of works that meet the criteria of originality and fixation occurs automatically at the moment of their creation: 'No registration of a work or any other special formalisation thereof, nor performance of any other formalities shall be required' for the existence or validity of copyright (Ukraine, 1993, Art. 11(2)).

However, legislation of many countries encourages copyright holders to observe some formalities, such as placing the copyright symbol (the © sign) on every copy of the work, registration and deposition of a copy of the work with a specially designated governmental institution. In the USA, for instance, such designated institution is the US Copyright Office, a branch of the Library of Congress.

Duration

Copyright subsists for a variety of lengths in different jurisdictions. International treaties do prescribe protection terms, but those terms are the minimums allowed. The duration of copyright can depend on several factors, such as the category of work, whether the work has been published or not, and whether the work was created by an individual or a company. In most of the world, the standard duration of copyright is the life of the author plus either 50 or 70 years (in the case of works of joint authorship, 70 years from the death of the last surviving co-author).

Establishing whether the term of protection has lapsed is not as straightforward as it may seem. The duration and requirements for copyright validity are subject to change by legislation and since the early 20th century there have been a number of considerable changes in legislation in many countries, which can make determining the copyright duration in a given country difficult. Thus, in the USA, there used to be a requirement of copyright renewal after the first 28 years. As a result, determining whether a work first published in the USA between 1923 and 1963 has entered the public domain involves consulting the Catalog of Copyright Entries published by the US Copyright Office (Public Domain Sherpa, 2013).

Who holds the copyright?

Establishing who exactly holds the copyright is the point of departure for copyright clearance: only after the author(s) or other copyright holder(s) have been established can they be approached to obtain permission to use their work. The copyright holder is not necessarily the author, for the copyright can be transferred wholly (assigned) or partially (licensed).

Moreover, economic (but not moral) rights in a work made in the course of an employee's duties, known as work for hire, belong to the employer by default, while the copyright in a work authored by a freelancer can, by contract, be fully retained by the author. The duration of copyright protection for a work for hire can be different from the standard one. Thus, in the USA, it spans for 100 years after the year of creation or 75 years after the year of publication, whichever expires first (USA, 1976, §302(c)).

The employer can well be a government, in which case the works resulting from the employee's activities are normally not entitled to copyright protection. The works of the US federal government, for instance, fall outside copyright protection (USA, 1976, §105). At the same time, the UK copyright statute envisages Crown (for works of the executive bodies of the UK and other Commonwealth realms) and parliamentary (for works of the British and the Scottish parliaments) copyright (UK 1988, ss. 163–67), both of which are usually waived or not enforced.

Irrespective of their copyright status, unless there are intellectual property rights of third parties, secrecy or confidentiality issues involved, documents generated by government agencies or government-controlled entities in the EU member states must be made available for re-use for a cost-based fee. Under the conditions set by the directive on the re-use of public sector information (European Union, 2003), public sector bodies may not enter into exclusive arrangements with individual re-users, unless exclusivity is necessary to cover costs of providing services in the public interest. Such services may include libraries (with the exception of university libraries), museums and archives providing public access to their digitised collections.

If the rightholder(s) cannot be established or located and thus contacted for copyright clearance purposes, one is dealing with the orphan works phenomenon. A great number of works around the world are orphan works and the uncertainty about their legal status stifles their preservation and dissemination, including that by virtue of memory institutions' digitisation projects. To address the problem, a special EU Directive (European Union, 2012) provided for a copyright exception, whereby publicly accessible libraries, educational establishments, museums, archives, film or audio heritage institutions and public service broadcasters may digitise orphan works and make them publicly available online after a diligent search does not yield the identity or location of the copyright holder(s). Two legislative bills to the same effect have been considered by the US Congress, but without success. In the USA, there are even calls for the restoration of the mandatory copyright registration to ease the search of the rightsholders. Although such a radical measure is hardly feasible, the need for an efficient way to identify and locate the rightsholders underscores the importance of metadata and rights management information (IFPI, 2003).

What cannot be done without the copyright holder's permission?

The main function of copyright as a legal construct is to ensure the protection of copyright holders (authors or other persons holding copyright) against unauthorised use of their works. This protection is achieved by declaring illegal any form of economic exploitation and derogatory treatment of works without consent of the copyright holder. Correspondingly, there are two categories of rights vested in copyright holders: economic rights and moral rights. While economic rights can be transferred, moral ones cannot (but usually can be waived in common law jurisdictions) (UK, 1988, s. 87; USA, 1976, § 106A).

Copyright holders have the exclusive rights to reproduction, adaptation, distribution, public performance or display, to communicate or to make works available to the public. Authors (but not other copyright holders) also enjoy rights 'to claim authorship of the work and to object to any distortion, mutilation or other modification of, or other derogatory action in relation to, the said work, which would be prejudicial to his honor or reputation' (WIPO, 1979, Art. 6bis). In essence, copyright is a temporary, limited monopoly, giving the monopolist a right to authorise or prohibit certain uses of the work. A use without authorisation constitutes a 'copyright infringement'.

Memory institutions can infringe on somebody's copyright in many ways, most obviously through unauthorised distribution. 'When a public library adds a work to its collection, lists the work in its index or catalog system, and makes the work available to the borrowing or browsing public, it has completed all the steps necessary for distribution to the public' (*Hotaling* v. *Church of Latter Day Saints* [1997] 203).

Unauthorised reproduction (making copies) and adaptation (creating derivative works) are also an issue for memory institutions. Whereas 'specific acts of reproduction made by publicly accessible libraries, educational establishments or museums, or by archives, which are not for direct or indirect economic or commercial advantage' (Malta, 2000, Art. 9(1)(d)) are permissible without licence, making derivative works, which can result from 'the adaptation, the arrangement and any other alteration' (Malta, 2000, Art. 7(1)(e)) by the same institutions is not.

Memory institutions possess a great number of copies for the simple reason that many of the works cannot be preserved and presented to users directly because of their character and form of expression. Such works which are fixed in traditional two- or three-dimensional forms are available to users only thanks to images resulting from photographing or filming them, scanning or using similar techno-logical processes. This applies to oral, dramatic and choreographic works, pantomimes and pictorial works, such as paintings, graphics, engravings, sculptures and architecture, and scientific works, such as illustrations, maps, schemes and charts.

Moreover, copying works is often the only way to prevent their deterioration or to replace them. Countless literary, musical, audiovisual, photographic and other kinds of works were saved by microfilming and other copying techniques. These days, the copying technique of choice is digitisation. After being transferred to a digital format, the originals are placed under special storage conditions, while the digital copies are made available to the public. Copying for preservation and replacement purposes is specifically allowed under US copyright law (USA, 1976, §108).

Whether the results of digitisation constitute derivative works depends on whether they meet the originality criterion. The originality of digitisation can consist in a creative recast of images, correction of the original defects, or a change in colours (colourisation) used in the restoration of old photographs and films. A purely mechanical transfer to a digital format, even if it involves image cropping or reframing, does not result in a derivative work. What is more, excessive editing of the resulting image can amount to an infringement of the author's moral rights.

Collective works should be treated with particular care, for the bundle of rights subsisting in them is usually complex, multi-layered and often includes neighbouring (related) rights – the rights of performers, phonogram producers and broadcasting organisations. Unless the rights in contributions to a collective work have been transferred to a single person, such as a producer, such rights have to be cleared individually.

For decades, copyright holders tolerated unauthorised yet legal acts of reproduction and distribution happening in libraries and other memory institutions, since those acts did not pose significant threat to their markets. The advent of the internet changed that. Nowadays, memory institutions are capable of communicating or making works available to the public over information networks, which makes them competitors to the copyright holders and destroys markets for licensed copies. This is why the copyright lobby made sure the use of works such as software, multimedia products, music, movies, databases and so on, including their reproduction on a magnetic or optical disk, uploading via the internet to another disk (server) or storage in computer memory and their subsequent distribution or offering access to them to an unlimited number of persons, can be done legally only after obtaining a licence.

The only exception was made for instances of 'communication to the public, for the purpose of research or private study, to individual members of the public by dedicated terminals on the premises of (memory institutions) of works and other subject matter, not subject to purchase or licensing terms, which are contained in their collections' (Malta, 2000, Art. 9(1)(v)). The 'other subject matter' here means a non-original database or an object of neighbouring (related) rights.

A licence is an authorisation to use a work and constitutes a contract between a copyright holder and a user. The copyright holder cannot limit by licence the users' behaviour necessary for normal exploitation of the work. In the case of a database, for instance, a licence cannot limit 'the performance of those acts which are normally necessary in order that the licensed user obtains access to the contents of the database and normal use thereof, in respect of the whole or part of the database which the user is licensed to use' (Malta, 2000, Art. 9(1)(w)).

One way of using a licence is to waive thereby some or all the rights belonging to the copyright holder. Despite popular belief, initiatives like Open Source or Creative Commons (CC) are not based on rejection of copyright, but on using it smartly: open source and CC licences allow copyright holders to define conditions under which others may use a work and to specify what types of use are permitted. Thus, there are six pre-set types of CC licences available. These are based on copyright holders' stipulations, such as whether they are willing to allow modifications to the work, to permit the creation of derivative works and to permit commercial use of the work (Creative Commons, 2010).

The types of uses copyright holders cannot limit by law, they can limit by technology. A growing number of technological measures are being used by copyright holders to restrict the types of uses of their works. Such measures, collectively known as technological protection measures, are part of, and often confused with, the more general term digital rights management, which includes all means of managing the use of works, including technological ones. Whether a particular digital rights management measure includes technological protection measures or not, it often requires users to identify themselves and allows tracking user behaviour (Cavoukian, 2002). In other words, digital rights management often involves looking into who reads, watches or listens to what. This brings privacy into the picture.

Privacy

Why privacy is relevant

The information embedded in artefacts, such as letters, diaries or photographs, stored by memory institutions, as well as the instances of consulting that information, is something that people usually prefer not to share with others. This human behaviour trait necessitated laws protecting privacy, famously defined as 'the right to be let alone' (Warren and Brandeis, 1890, 193).

The role of the memory institution as a guardian of privacy is thus twofold. First, the privacy of those whose personal data is contained in the artefacts merits protection. Whereas data stored at the traditional archives of the filing cabinets type was relatively hard to access by an outsider and to correlate with each other, information and communications technology makes it easy to pull it together to form a profile, a rather accurate physical, psychological and social portrait of a person. 'An individual may give out bits of information in different contexts, each transfer appearing innocuous. However, the information can be aggregated and could prove to be invasive of the private life when combined with other information. It is the totality of information about a person and how it is used that poses the greatest threat to privacy' (Solove, 2001, 1452).

On the other hand, the privacy of those who consult the artefacts calls for protection, since analysing what kind of materials a person consulted can give a pretty good idea as to what the person's tastes, preferences, opinions and political allegiances are. This is the type of data both the private sector and the government are after. To make matters worse, 'Big Brother' gets increasingly more personal data from the myriads of 'little brothers', both public and private. Unfortunately, memory institutions can be 'little brothers', too. For instance, there are numerous examples of governments' attempts to obtain information on what citizens read from libraries. The USA has a long history of the authorities forcing librarians into the role of informants (Starr, 2004), the latest occurrences of which were under the pretext of the 'war on terror' (Airoldi, 2005).

Initially, law protected 'only the physical interference of life and property', but eventually law has come to a 'recognition of man's spiritual nature, of his feelings and his intellect' (Solove, Rotenberg and Schwartz, 2006, 9–10). This gave rise to legal protection of the privacy of information generated in different areas of human activities – medicine, finances, politics, telecommunications, and so on – besides physical privacy. These types of privacy are collectively known as informational privacy, which, correspondingly, includes medical privacy, financial privacy, political privacy, telecommunications privacy, etc.

Personal data protection

Informational privacy is afforded through legal protection provided for in law to personal data, understood as 'any information relating to an identified or identifiable individual ("data subject")' (Council of Europe, 1981, Art. 2(a)). Owing to the Council of Europe and EU membership, laws on personal data protection in Europe share a considerable degree of uniformity. In the EU member states, such uniformity has been further re-enforced by the adoption of the general data protection regulation that replaced the data protection directive (European Union, 1995) on 25 May 2018.

Under the regulation, a natural person is considered identifiable, if he or she 'can be identified, directly or indirectly, in particular by reference to an identifier such as a name, an identification number, location data, an online identifier or to one or more factors specific to the physical, physiological, genetic, mental, economic, cultural or social identity of that natural person' (European Union, 2016, Art. 4(1)). Accordingly, data contained in an archived document bearing an individual's name or some other identifier (ID card number, social security or tax ID number, etc.), as well as data contained in a book circulation record stored by a library, would be considered personal data in the legal sense. However, irrevocably de-identified or 'rendered anonymous' data, such as internet log files not containing users' names, ID numbers or other identifiers, would not constitute personal data. Hence, genuinely 'anonymising' personal data is a way to avoid the data protection legislation's applicability to a data processing operation (European Union, 2016, Recital 26).

'Anonymisation' should not be confused with 'pseudonymisation' – 'the processing of personal data in such a manner that the personal data can no longer be attributed to a specific data subject without the use of additional information, provided that such additional information is kept separately and is subject to technical and organisational measures to ensure that the personal data are not attributed to an identified or identifiable natural person'. 'Pseudomised' data, in contrast to 'anonymised' data, can still be re-identified or de-anonymised (Pastukhov, 2014, 1274).

A 'physical person' is normally understood as a living human being. 'Information relating to dead individuals is, therefore, in principle, not to be considered as personal data subject to the rules of the [data protection legislation]' (Article 29 Data Protection Working Party, 2007, 22). This is in line with the principle of Roman Law 'known as *actio personalis moritur cum persona* – personal causes of action die with the person – and although this principle has been whittled away at in certain contexts, it still stands as a relatively entrenched principle in relation to post mortem privacy claims' (Edwards, 2013, 3). There is some flexibility to this rule, however, and such EU member states as Bulgaria and Estonia offer a limited *post mortem* protection to personal data, while in all the member states personal data of the deceased can be protected indirectly in a number of ways (e.g., by medical secrecy laws) (Harbinja, 2013, 26–7).

'Processing of personal data' means 'any operation or set of operations which is performed on personal data or on sets of personal data, whether or not by automated means, such as collection, recording, organisation, structuring, storage, adaptation or alteration, retrieval, consultation, use, disclosure by transmission, dissemination or otherwise making available, alignment or combination, restriction, erasure or destruction' (European Union, 2016, Art. 4(2)). Nearly all, if not all, of the enumerated acts form core activities of memory institutions. Even the mere act of holding (mentioned above as 'storage') personal data is a regulated activity under EU law.

If a memory institution operates independently, this makes it a 'data controller', a 'natural or legal person, public authority, agency or other body which, alone or jointly with others, determines the purposes and means of the processing of personal data' (European Union, 2016, Art. 4(7)). If the memory institution is an integral part or acts as agent of another entity, it has a status of a 'data processor', 'a natural or legal person, public authority, agency or other body which processes personal data on behalf of the controller' (European Union, 2016, Art. 4(8)).

The regulation establishes six 'data quality' principles, according to which the data controller must ensure that personal data:

- is processed 'lawfully, fairly and in a transparent manner in relation to the data subject' (the 'lawfulness, fairness and transparency' principle)
- is collected 'specified, explicit and legitimate purposes and not further processed in a manner that is incompatible with those purposes', whereas 'further processing for archiving purposes in the public interest, scientific or historical research purposes or statistical purposes shall . . . not be considered to be incompatible with the initial purposes' (the 'purpose limitation' principle)
- is 'adequate, relevant and limited to what is necessary in relation to the purposes for which they are processed' (the 'data minimisation' principle)
- is 'accurate and, where necessary, kept up to date', while 'every reasonable step must be taken to ensure that personal data that are inaccurate, having regard to the purposes for which they are processed, are erased or rectified without delay' (the 'accuracy' principle)
- is 'kept in a form which permits identification of data subjects for no longer than is necessary for the purposes for which the personal data are processed', whereas 'personal data may be stored for longer periods insofar as the personal data will be processed solely for archiving purposes in the public interest, scientific or historical research purposes or statistical purposes . . . subject to implementation of the appropriate technical and organisational measures' (the 'storage limitation principle')
- is 'processed in a manner that ensures appropriate security of the personal data, including protection against unauthorised or unlawful processing and against accidental loss, destruction or damage, using appropriate technical or organisational measures' (the 'integrity and confidentiality' principle) (European Union, 2016, Art. 5(1)).

What is particularly relevant to memory institutions is that 'further processing' and storage of personal data 'for longer periods' is allowed for 'archiving purposes in the public interest, scientific or historical research purposes' provided 'appropriate safeguards' are in place:

> Those safeguards shall ensure that technical and organisational measures are in place in particular in order to ensure respect for the principle of data minimisation. Those measures may include pseudonymisation provided that those purposes can be fulfilled in that manner. Where those purposes can be fulfilled by further processing which does not permit or no longer permits the identification of data subjects, those purposes shall be fulfilled in that manner.
>
> (European Union, 2016, Art. 89(1))

Personal data may be processed in the EU lawfully only if the data subject has indicated his or her 'freely given, specific, informed' consent to that (European Union, 2016, Art. 4(11)) or the processing is necessary to:

- perform 'a contract to which the data subject is party or in order to take steps at the request of the data subject prior to entering into a contract'
- comply with 'a legal obligation to which the controller is subject'
- protect the data subject's or another natural person's 'vital interests'
- perform a task 'in the public interest' or exercise an 'official authority vested in the controller'
- further 'the legitimate interests pursued by the controller or by a third party', unless the processing infringes 'the interests or fundamental rights and freedoms of the data subject' (European Union, 2016, Art. 6(1)).

Furthermore, the so-called 'sensitive data' enjoys an extra level of protection: 'Processing of personal data revealing racial or ethnic origin, political opinions, religious or philosophical beliefs, or trade union membership, and the processing of genetic data, biometric data for the purpose of uniquely identifying a natural person, data concerning health or data concerning a natural person's sex life or sexual orientation shall be prohibited', except where an exception, such as an 'explicit' consent of the data subject, applies (European Union, 2016, Art. 9).

The regulation requires that data subjects must be informed when data on them are processed. The notice must include the reasons why the data was collected, by whom and who will have access to the data (European Union, 2016, Arts. 13, 14). Data subjects must also be informed of their rights under the regulation, including the right to access data concerning them, the right to the rectification of inaccurate data, and the right to erasure (the 'right to be forgotten') (European Union, 2016, Arts. 16–17). These rights are necessary prerequisites to secure the individual's informational self-determination – the possibility to determine how data on them are processed by others. The right to erasure as provided for by the regulation is aimed at achieving this goal by imposing on the data controller two duties:

- the duty to erase 'without undue delay' personal data that the controller processes on legal grounds provided for in the regulation when these legal grounds disappear or become inapplicable
- the duty to, 'taking account of available technology and the cost of implementation . . . take reasonable steps, including technical measures, to inform controllers which are processing the personal data that the data subject has requested the erasure by such controllers of any links to, or copy or replication of, those personal data'.

None of these duties can be seen as creating a meaningful 'right to oblivion' – the right to object to a lawful data processing on grounds other than the data subject's consent (Pastukhov, 2013). However, the Court of Justice of the European Union in its famous decision (*Google Spain SL and Google Inc.* v. *Agencia Española de Protección de Datos and Mario Costeja González* [2014]), seems to have 'planted a seed' of such right (Bartolini and Siry, 2016, 235).

The regulation's right to erasure should not stand in the way of the people's 'right to know', even if processing some kinds of personal data can lead to the data subject's public humiliation or embarrassment. This is why the relevant rules of the regulation do not apply in cases when the processing is necessary, inter alia, 'for exercising the right of freedom of expression and information' and 'for archiving purposes in the public interest, scientific or historical research purposes or statistical purposes in accordance . . . in so far as the right [to erasure] is likely to render impossible or seriously impair the achievement of the objectives of that processing' (European Union, 2016, Art. 17(3)).

Besides providing for the data subject's private right of action, the directive requires each EU member state to set up a national data protection authority, an independent government agency with supervisory and enforcement powers in personal data protection. Some data protection authorities, such as the French Commission nationale de l'informatique et des libertés (CNIL) and the British Information Commissioner's Office, are rather proactive and often intervene in situations involving actual or potential privacy breaches. Several data protection authorities also require data controllers to file annual summaries of all personal data processing they perform, while CNIL requires prior declarations and even reserves the right to expressly authorise certain proposed data processing operations (Linklaters, 2013).

Conclusion

The launch and progress of such projects as Europeana (www.europeana.eu/ portal/en) or Digital Public Library of America (DPLA; https://dp.la/) attest to the popular demand for a cheap, fast and efficient way to access vast collections of memory institutions. For these digital collections to avoid legal obstacles, they have to be compliant with legal requirements applicable to their operations.

Copyright is one of the most important areas of law related to digital archiving. As long as digitisation is increasingly used by memory institutions for preserving and delivering information on artefacts held in their collections, issues related to copyright protection will be of growing importance. National laws and international accords contribute a considerable degree of legal certainty to memory institutions' operations, but many uncertainties still persist, for example, around the status of orphan works or protectability of metadata.

Another area of law of utmost importance to digital archiving is privacy. Privacy law has permeated many spheres of human activities. Accordingly, the types of privacy, besides physical privacy, have come to include informational privacy and its subsets: medical privacy, financial privacy, political privacy, and so on. These developments made memory institutions guardians of privacy for both those whose personal data is contained in the materials in their possession and those who consult the same materials. Data protection law is a rapidly evolving area, which still has many loopholes to close, such as those surrounding post mortem privacy or the 'right to be forgotten'.

With the growth in popularity of publicly accessible digital archives, memory institutions will be increasingly exposed to legal risks by running afoul of privacy or copyright laws, or otherwise. Devising a legal risk management plan is therefore advisable. When in doubt as to the legal consequences of certain actions related to digitisation, professional legal advice should be sought.

References

Airoldi, J. (2005) Librarian's Brush with FBI Shapes Her View of the USA PATRIOT Act, *USA Today*, 17 May, www.usatoday.com/news/opinion/editorials/ 2005-05-17-librarian-edit_x.htm.

Article 29 Data Protection Working Party (2007) *Opinion 4/2007 on the Concept of Personal Data*, adopted on 20 June, 01248/07/EN WP 136, http://ec.europa.eu/justice/policies/privacy/docs/wpdocs/2007/ wp136_en.pdf.

Bartolini, C. and Siry, L. (2016) The Right to be Forgotten in the Light of the Consent of the Data Subject, *Computer Law & Security Review*, **32** (2), 218–37, http://dx.doi.org/10.1016/j.clsr.2016.01.005.

Berenboom, A. (2005) *Le Nouveau Droit d'Auteur et les Droits Voisins*, 3rd edn, Éditions Larcier.

Bridy, A. (2012) Coding Creativity: copyright and the artificially intelligent author, *Technology Law Review*, **5**, 1–28.

Bulgaria (1993) Law on Copyright and Neighbouring Rights, *State Gasette* No. 56/1993; amended No. 63/1994, No. I 0/1 998, No. 28/2000, No. 77/2002, www.wipo.int/wipolex/en/text.jsp?file_id=125323.

Cavoukian, A. (2002) *Privacy and Digital Rights Management (DRM): an oxymoron?*, Information and Privacy Commissioner of Ontario, www.ic.gc.ca/app/oca/crd/dcmnt.do?id=753&lang=eng.

Council of Europe (1981) Convention for the Protection of Individuals with Regard to Automatic Processing of Personal Data, Strasbourg, 28

January, http://conventions.coe.int/Treaty/en/Treaties/Html/108.htm.

Coyle, K. (2013) Metadata and Copyright, *Library Journal*, 28 February,
http://lj.libraryjournal.com/2013/02/opinion/peer-to-peer-review/
metadata-and-copyright-peer-to-peer-review/#_.

Creative Commons (2010) *About the Licenses*,
http://creativecommons.org/licenses/.

Edwards, L. (2013) Post Mortem Privacy, editorial, *SCRIPTed*, **10** (1), 1–6,
http://script-ed.org/wp-content/uploads/2013/04/editorial.pdf.

European Union (1995) Directive 95/46/EC of the European Parliament and
of the Council of 24 October 1995 on the Protection of Individuals with
regard to the Processing of Personal Data and on the Free Movement of
such Data, *Official Journal*, L 281, 23 November, 31, http://eur-lex.
europa.eu/legal-content/en/TXT/?uri=CELEX%3A31995L0046.

European Union (2003) Directive 2003/98/EC of the European Parliament
and of the Council of 17 November 2003 on the Re-use of Public Sector
Information, *Official Journal*, L 345, 31 December, 90 (amended by
Directive 2013/37/EU of the European Parliament and of the Council of
26 June 2013, *Official Journal*, L 175, 27 June 2013, 1), http://eur-
lex.europa.eu/LexUriServ/LexUriServ.do?uri=
CONSLEG:2003L0098:20130717:EN:PDF.

European Union (2012) Directive 2012/28/EU of the European Parliament
and of the Council of 25 October 2012 on Certain Permitted Uses of
Orphan Works, *Official Journal*, L 299, 27 October, 5, http://eur-lex.
europa.eu/LexUriServ/LexUriServ.do?uri=OJ:L:2012:299:0005:0012:
EN:PDF.

European Union (2016) Regulation (EU) 2016/679 of the European
Parliament and of the Council of 27 April 2016 on the Protection of
Natural Persons with regard to the Processing of Personal Data and on
the Free Movement of such Data, and Repealing Directive 95/46/EC
(General Data Protection Regulation), *Official Journal*, L 119, 4 May, 1,
http://eur-lex.europa.eu/legal-content/en/TXT/?uri=
CELEX%3A32016R0679.

Feist Publications, Inc. v. *Rural Telephone Service Co.* [1991] 499 US 340; 111 S.
Ct. 1282.

Google Spain SL and Google Inc. v. *Agencia Española de Protección de Datos and
Mario Costeja González* [2014] Decision C-131/12, ECLI:EU:C:2014:317.

Harbinja, E. (2013) Does the EU Data Protection Regime Protect Post-
Mortem Privacy and What Could Be the Potential Alternatives?,

SCRIPTed, **10** (1), 19–38, http://script-ed.org/wp-content/uploads/
2013/04/harbinja.pdf.

Hotaling v. *Church of Latter Day Saints* [1997] 118 F.3d 199 (4th Cir.).

IFPI (2003) The WIPO Treaties: protection of rights management
information, International Federation of the Phonographic Industry,
www.ifpi.org/content/library/wipo-treaties-rights-management-
information.pdf.

Linklaters (2013) Data Protected – France, National Regulatory Authority,
https://clientsites.linklaters.com/Clients/dataprotected/Pages/
France.aspx#nra.

Malta (2000) Copyright Act, in *Laws of Malta*, Chapter 415,
www.justiceservices.gov.mt/DownloadDocument.aspx?app=
lom&itemid=8881&l=1.

Pastukhov, O. (2013) The Right to Oblivion: what's in the name?, *Computer
& Telecommunications Law Review*, **19** (1), 17–23.

Pastukhov, O. (2014) Legal Aspects of CCTV Data De-identification, in
*[Proceedings of the] 37th International Convention on Information and
Communication Technology, Electronics and Microelectronics (MIPRO)*,
1273–77, http://ieeexplore.ieee.org/document/6859763/.

Public Domain Sherpa (2013) Copyright Renewal: when it had to happen,
or else, www.publicdomainsherpa.com/copyright-renewal.html.

Rodríguez-Doncel, V., Santos, C., Casanovas, P. and Gómez-Pérez, A. (2016)
Legal Aspects of Linked Data – the European framework, *Computer Law
& Security Review*, **32** (6), 799–813,
http://dx.doi.org/10.1016/j.clsr.2016.07.005.

Solove, D. J. (2001) Privacy and Power: computer databases and metaphors
for information privacy, *Stanford Law Review*, **53** (6), 1393–1462.

Solove, D. J., Rotenberg, M. and Schwartz, P. M. (2006) *Privacy, Information,
and Technology*, Aspen Publishers.

Starr, J. (2004) Libraries and National Security: an historical review, *First
Monday*, **9** (12),
http://firstmonday.org/ojs/index.php/fm/article/view/1198/1118.

Ukraine (1993) Law of Ukraine 'On Copyright and Related Rights'
(Vidomosti Verkhovnoyi Rady Ukrayiny (VVR), 1994, No. 13, 64) (with
later amendments), www.wipo.int/wipolex/en/text.jsp?file_id=142655.

UK (1988) Copyright, Designs and Patents Act 1988,
www.legislation.gov.uk/ukpga/1988/48.

USA (1976) Copyright Act of 1976, as amended, US Code, Title 17, §§101–

810. www.law.cornell.edu/copyright/copyright.table.html.

USA (1995) *Information Infrastructure Task Force, Intellectual Property and the National Information Infrastructure: the report of the Working Group on Intellectual Property,*
http://groups.csail.mit.edu/mac/classes/6.805/articles/int-prop/nii-report-sept95.txt..

Warren, S. and Brandeis, L. (1890) The Right to Privacy, *Harvard Law Review,* **4** (5), 193–220.

WIPO (1979) Berne Convention for the Protection of Literary and Artistic Works, Paris Act of 24 July 1979, as amended on 28 September 1979, World Intellectual Property Organization,
www.wipo.int/treaties/en/text.jsp?file_id=283698.

5

Scientific information policies in the European context

Carla Basili

Introduction and background

The discourses on knowledge production and knowledge dissemination have traditionally been dealt with separately, as referring to two different systems: the 'science system' and the 'scholarly communication system'. Yet, this separation was even more reinforced by being the processes carried out by the two communities: scientists as knowledge production agents, information professionals as knowledge dissemination agents (Basili, 2009).

This same distinction applies also to policy issues and measures, conceived independently for scientific research from one side, and dissemination and access to scientific information from the other (Basili, 2010). Correspondingly, such a dichotomy reverberates throughout two basic threads of literature: one dealing with the 'knowledge society' (e.g. David and Foray, 2002; Sörlin and Vessuri, 2007) and one dealing with the 'information society' (e.g. EC, 1999; Webster, 2006).

In recent decades, such clear separation is largely blurred, as a consequence of techno-economic forces and factors affecting knowledge dissemination, primarily the internet and the entrepreneurial climate in research and development. To summarise in a nutshell, the two discourses on the information society and knowledge society can be interpreted and analysed as converging towards the discourse on the 'knowledge economy', with major policy implications for scientific information, since, at the same time, an economic logic increasingly enters into the domain of knowledge dissemination.

This interdependent connection appears evident in the policy documents from the European Commission and the European Parliament released since the Lisbon Council of March 2000, and effectively expressed in European Commission COM(2012) 392 final: 'Knowledge is the currency of the new economy' (EC, 2012a).

Focusing the attention on economic pressures more than on technological opportunities, in this chapter a short account will be given on how the transformation from academic science to entrepreneurial science has been theorised in the research policy literature.

Theoretical literature about research policy is abundant and multifaceted, nevertheless, reference here is made to the concepts 'Mertonian norms', 'mode 2 knowledge production model' and 'Triple Helix', which have a significant impact on the rationale of this chapter.

In 1942, in his essay 'The Normative Structure of Science', Merton formalised the scientific behaviour of scientists, identifying a set of principles that – despite having been criticised and challenged – still make for a valid reference framework in order to outline and interpret the cultural background that informs the processes of production and circulation of scientific knowledge within the context of academic science.

Mertonian norms are usually referred to in the literature by using the acronym CUDOS, deriving from the initial letter of each of the norms:

- *communalism*: sharing scientific results for the good of science, which means that all the elements that make up scientific production are in the public domain; therefore, in Merton's view, knowledge is a public good
- *universalism*: science does not have territorial or geopolitical borders, and no prejudice is accepted in relation to the nationality, race, religion, social class or personal characteristics of the individual members of the scientific community
- *disinterestedness*: individual interest is subordinate to the common interest of science
- *organised scepticism*: scientific progress is independent from political, religious or economic interests.

In later writings, Merton added the principle of originality, which refers to the high value attributed by the scientific system to the original fathering of ideas and scientific results.

Conversely, industrial research strictly abides by well-defined rules, dictated by the private organisations that finance the researchers' work contracts. This means that industrial research pursues objectives and obeys priorities that are ultimately set by the market. This set up favours fields of investigation having short-term or, at the most, mid-term applications, to the detriment of exploratory or basic research, which yields long-term results whose applicability is not foreseeable or measurable *ab initio*.

Industrial research is fuelled by the same base of knowledge that academic science feeds on but, differently from it, it strictly controls the circulation of research results by means of patents and licences of use.

The logic underlying industrial research was formalised by Ziman (1995) through a set of principles that pit themselves against Merton's ethos, by opposing the concept of proprietary to that of communalist, that of local to that of universal, that of authoritarian to that of disinterested, that of commissioned to that of original, and that of expert to that of sceptical, as illustrated in Figure 5.1. The acronym CUDOS is used for the Mertonian model and PLACE is used for the Ziman model.

Academic science	Industrial science
Communalist	Proprietary
Universal	Local
Disinterested	Authoritarian
Original	Commissioned
Sceptical	Expert

Figure 5.1 *The synonyms CUDOS and PLACE*

To explain the so-called 'third mission' of the university (the mission of economic and social role, in addition to the traditional roles of research and education) two influential models have been developed:

• the 'Triple Helix' model of university–industry–government relations (Etzkowitz and Leydesdorff, 1998) in which university 'can play an enhanced role in innovation in increasingly knowledge-based societies'

- the Mode 2 knowledge production model (Gibbons et al., 1994.) implying there is an interaction among a plurality of actors for the production of knowledge (university, industry and other 'knowledge producers').

Both the Triple Helix and the Mode 2 knowledge production models have a significant implication for knowledge circulation through the process of knowledge transfer, in its different forms: it is evident there is a need to juxtapose processes of knowledge transfer with the traditional processes of knowledge sharing through scholarly communication (Basili, 2013).

These theoretical developments conform and systematise real processes and changes resulting from the convergence of events, interests and trends that occur, as will be outlined below.

Research and development at the core of a pan-European economic strategy

Alongside these theoretical developments, in the European Union mature and material facts, decisions and positions aim to meet the demands of the moment. In particular, the reference context of the European Commission policy strategies is determined by some basic factors:

- the establishment of a European research area (EC, 2000) as it was originally expected by the Lisbon Strategy: 'a unified research area open to the world based on the Internal Market, in which researchers, scientific knowledge and technology circulate freely and through which the Union and its member states strengthen their scientific and technological bases, their competitiveness and their capacity to collectively address grand challenges' (EC, 2012a)
- the idea of scientific research as an element for growth and economic development: 'The central role of research was recognised by the Lisbon European Council of 23–24 March 2000 which set the European Union a new strategic goal for the next decade: to become the most competitive and dynamic knowledge-based economy in the world' (EP, 2006)
- the move of the centre of gravity of scientific research from public

to private influence: 'In line with the Lisbon Strategy, the Barcelona European Council of 15–16 March 2002 agreed that overall spending on research and development ('RTD') and innovation in the Union should be increased with the aim of approaching 3% of GDP by 2010, two-thirds of which should come from the private sector' (EP, 2006).

These are the keys to a reading of the policies for knowledge sharing and knowledge transfer that will be shown in the next paragraphs. In order to better understand the current situation, however, it may be useful to provide a brief historical account of the evolution of policies for scientific information.

Research and scientific information: historical background

The international discourse on scientific information policies has been evolving since the mid-1900s and it has been characterised by a sequence of crucial stages: it began with raising awareness about the importance of scientific information, then it dealt with infrastructural solutions of an institutional and technical nature, and finally it came to consider scientific information as a socio-economic good. In each phase, it should be emphasised, scientific information has constantly been seen as a universal heritage of humanity and, consequently, the main objective in the long or mid-term has been that of supporting not only the development of national information policies but also, and above all, their harmonisation at the international level.

Therefore, it is possible to pinpoint a number of milestone events in the international discourse on scientific information policies – or, more precisely, on scientific and technical information, as the literature has been calling this field for decades.

The Royal Society Scientific Information Conference, held in London in 1948, represented the first signal of awareness about the strategic value of scientific and technical information – which was developing in the years after World War 2 – and explored all the problematic issues concerning scientific information in an extensive and all-round way.

Around ten years later, the International Conference on Scientific Information (ICSI) tried to deal with similar issues. The conference took place in Washington in 1958 and was organised by the National

Science Foundation, the US National Academy of Sciences and the American Documentation Institute – whose name was then changed to American Society for Information Science. The proceedings of the ICSI revolved around the following topics of discussion:

Literature and reference needs of scientists

Function and effectiveness of Abstracting and Indexing (A&I) services

Effectiveness of Monographs, Compendia, and Specialized Centers

Organization of information for storage and search: comparative characteristics of existing systems

Organization of information for storage and retrospective search: intellectual problems and equipment considerations

Organization of information for storage and retrospective search: possibility for a general theory

Responsibilities of Government, Societies, Universities, and industry for improved information services and research.

(National Research Council, 1959)

A few years later, the Committee for Scientific Research of the Organisation for Economic Co-operation and Development (OECD) addressed the issue of science information policy in a 1962 report, in which information is analysed from the economic point of view and strictly linked to economic development, since the latter is seen as depending not only on scientific research but also on the effective and rapid transmission of research results (Godin, 2008; OECD, 1962).

In the 1970s, UNESCO took on a leading international role and tried to achieve the double objective of setting up the UN International Scientific Information System (UNISIST) and developing and harmonising national information policies in member states through the National Information System (NATIS).

The UNISIST International Programme for the Exchange of Scientific and Technical Information was initiated in 1972, following a discussion concerning its feasibility, which lasted for a few years. Its objective was to develop 'co-ordinated and sustained international action in order to facilitate transfer of scientific and technical information for the economic development of nations', in the belief that 'specialised knowledge is an instrument of social change and provides a source of power for social and economic development' (UNESCO, 1979).

In 1977 UNESCO merged together the UNISIST and NATIS programmes into the General Information Programme (*Programme général d'information*; PGI), which focused on meeting a set of objectives defined in the chapter 'Transfer and exchange of information' of the first UNESCO Medium-Term Plan for 1977–1982 (UNESCO, 1988):

> Promotion of the formulation of information policies and plans (national, regional and international)
>
> Promotion and dissemination of methods, norms and standards for information handling
>
> Contribution to the development of information infrastructures
>
> Contribution to the development of specialised information systems in the fields of education, culture and communication, and natural and social sciences
>
> Promotion of the training and education of specialists in and users of information.

Once again, as for the NATIS and UNISIST programmes, in UNESCO's view information policies are of highest priority.

After four decades, the view has changed and somehow broadened, to acknowledge the demands of the economy of information and the new economy of science. However, no attempt at systematisation having international scope, comparable to that carried out by UNESCO for scientific information in the 1970s, has so far been produced for information as a whole.

The programmes were devised to target the problems that were most pressing in the 1970s and UNESCO proposed to solve them with the technologies available then. Nowadays, some of the problems that were crucial then are no longer so and some of the solutions then proposed might appear naive, in light of the current technological developments, as pointed out by Hjørland, Søndergaard and Andersen, who revised the UNISIST model (Hjørland, Søndergaard and Andersen, 2003).

For the purposes of this chapter, the proposal made by UNESCO in those years is still significant today in relation to its political logic – the conception of information and knowledge as goods to be shared – rather than for what concerns the technological operating details proposed for the implementation of the science information system.

In October 2000 the PGI was merged into the Information for All Programme – still in place today – with a strategic plan for 2008–2013, including a coherent set of goals, among which the following come first in the list:

- to 'develop and maintain an observatory on information policies and strategies'
- to 'draw on existing Member State resources and on the expertise of Member States and its multi-stakeholder partners wherever possible, but where there are gaps, develop new resources for Member States to use in preparing their own national information policy frameworks'
- to 'develop for this purpose an overall comprehensive information and knowledge policy framework, covering all the channels for gathering and distributing information, and complemented by policy frameworks in five priority areas – information for development, information literacy, information preservation, information ethics and information accessibility' (IFAP, 2007).

The document stated: 'The goal set in this plan is to mainstream "information" into national public policy agendas' (IFAP, 2007).

In the same year the European Commission and the European Parliament launched the policy initiative 'eEurope: an information society for all', included in the above mentioned Lisbon Strategy, with a perspective more technological than informational (EC, 1999).

We cannot overlook that the goal of developing a scientific information policy has been a constant priority in the international debate over the last 50 years; however, it has proven to be an elusive quarry, considering that in a long-term document such as the Information for All Programme strategic plan (2008–2013) this goal is still listed among those to be achieved.

The Commission's policies on scientific information since 2006

Against this background, the European Commission (EC) interest in scientific information gained momentum from January 2006 onwards, with a 'Study on the Economic and Technical Evolution of the Scientific

Publication Markets in Europe' (EC, 2006a) followed by a public consultation (from 31 March to 15 June 2006) addressed to individual researchers, academic organisations, libraries, information organisations and publishers. Results from the 2006 consultation (EC, 2006b) have provided the basis for the next communication on scientific information in the digital age: access, dissemination and preservation, where a whole paragraph states:

THE IMPORTANCE OF SCIENTIFIC INFORMATION
In order to become an increasingly *competitive knowledge-based economy*, Europe must improve the production of knowledge through research, its dissemination through education, and its application through innovation. All research builds on former work, and depends on scientists' possibilities to access and share scientific publications and *research data*. The rapid and widespread dissemination of research results can help *accelerate innovation* and avoid duplication of research efforts, although *some delay* for the first use by researchers or for *commercial purposes* can be justified.   (EC, 2007, 2, emphasis added)

Italics have been used to emphasise some terms which deserve to be briefly commented on, also in light of a comparison between the above views, dated 2007, and similar views expressed in 1948 at the (above mentioned) First International Scientific Information Conference, where the following was declared: 'Science rests upon its published record, and ready access to public scientific and technical information is a fundamental need for scientists everywhere.'

First, in 2007 the importance of scientific information was explicitly justified based on the link existing between the knowledge economy and Innovation, understood as the application (including commercial purposes) of the knowledge produced by research. This logic was completely absent in 1948, when technical-scientific information was conceived as remaining entirely within the province of the scientific community (scientists).

Another major difference between the two approaches is the shift from publications (published record), mentioned in 1948, to the broader concept of 'research results' expressed in 2007, which also includes (at least) research data along with publications.

The two stances present subtler references to economic aspects. The

1948 declaration referred to public scientific information, which undoubtedly meant non-confidential information but also information resulting from research financed through public funding. In 2007, explicit reference is made to the exploitation of research results for commercial purposes as well as to 'some delay' in their dissemination within the scientific community – it might be guessed, in order for the patenting process to be completed, since patenting regulations forbid publication before a patent is issued. On the contrary, in 1948, the need for ready access to public scientific information was asserted without compromise.

Explicit reference to the benefits expected from the public funding of research is also made in one of the most recent communications of the EC – COM(2012) 401 – which clearly outlines this strategy starting from its title: 'Towards Better Access to Scientific Information: Boosting the Benefits of Public Investments in Research' (EC, 2012c).

Lastly, the Opinion of the European Economic and Social Committee on COM(2012) 401 dispels all doubts when, in its first paragraph it states, 'Access to scientific information is an essential requirement for successful research and boosting innovation, and therefore for Europe's competitiveness as well' (EESC, 2012).

After five years from the first, a second consultation on scientific information in the digital age was launched in 2011 from the EC; this initiative 'builds on earlier policy developments in this area, and is being developed within the policy contexts of the EU Flagship Initiatives Innovation Union and Digital Agenda for Europe, and of the push for improved knowledge circulation in the European Research Area' (EC, 2011b). Results of this consultation formed the basis for the EC recommendation on access to and preservation of scientific information, C(2012) 4890 (EC, 2012b), whose content will be outlined in the next paragraphs.

EU policies for knowledge sharing

Open access

A large body of literature extensively addresses the open access issue in its different facets, therefore here is highlighted only a list of the milestones in the development of the European policies on open access:

- December 2006: European Research Advisory Board (EURAB) final report, *Scientific Publication: policy on open access*
- December 2006: European Research Council Scientific Council statement on open access
- September 2007: consultation on open access question (No. 21) of green paper *The European Research Area: new perspectives* (ERA green paper)
- December 2007: European Research Council Scientific Council Guidelines for Open Access
- July 2008: *Open Access Handbook,* joint publication by the EC and the German Commission for UNESCO
- August 2008: launch of open access pilot in FP7
- December 2010: official launch of FP7 project OpenAIRE
- February 2011: EC and FP7 project partners report *Open Access and Preservation in the European Research Area: paving the way towards a sound strategy*
- November 2011: proposal for open access in Horizon 2020
- December 2011: national open access and preservation policies in Europe
- January 2012: survey on open access in FP7
- October 2012: frequently asked questions on open access to publications and data in Horizon 2020
- March 2017: *Guidelines to the Rules on Open Access to Scientific Publications and Open Access to Research Data in Horizon 2020,* Version 3.2.

It is important to note the frequency and consistency of the various initiatives, as well as their different institutional provenance.

Open data – research data

Taking advantage of the current technological availability, the experimental research is able today to produce vast amounts of data that can feed more strands of future inquiry, if shared within the scientific community. In Borgman's words, 'researchers are producing an unprecedented deluge of data by using new methods and instrumentation. Others may wish to mine these data for new discoveries and innovations' (Borgman, 2012).

In the vision of the EC, scientific information includes literature and data as both constitute forms of research results, and therefore the recommendations issued for scientific information, such as open access and preservation, are constantly referring also to research data (see also Cragin et al., 2010).

Nevertheless, a number of initiatives (by the EC and other influential bodies) have been specifically devoted to research data and are listed below in chronological order:

- 2007 – OECD *Principles and Guidelines for Access to Research Data from Public Funding* (OECD, 2007)
- October 2010 – *Riding the Wave* (Wood et al., 2010)
- December 2011 – COM(2011) 882 final, *Open Data* (EC, 2011a)
- July 2013 – EC *Public Consultation on Open Research Data* (EC, 2013).

The consultation was addressed to the main stakeholders on research data (researchers, publishers, librarians, university staff and industry representatives) and based on five key questions:

- How can we define research data and what types of data should be open?
- How should the issue of data re-use be addressed?
- When and how does openness need to be limited?
- Where should research data be stored and made accessible?
- How can we enhance data awareness and a culture of sharing?

The report of the European Commission public consultation on open research data (EC, 2013) provides a detailed account of the outcomes of the consultation, to be used in policy definition.

The focus of this chapter is on the diverse kinds of scientific information, nevertheless, it is worth noticing a parallel line of policy actions by the EC, devoted to a vision on data and data management considered as economic factors. In fact, a diverse course of policy actions has been taken by the EC within the Digital Single Market Strategy, towards building a European data economy. Milestones of this strategy are the following initiatives launched on 10 January 2017:

- the release of COM(2017) 9 final on building a European data economy (EC, 2017a), with the Commission staff working document SWD (2017) 2 final on the free flow of data and emerging issues of the European data economy, accompanying COM(2017) 9 final (EC, 2017b)
- the launch of a public consultation on building a European data economy from 10 January to 26 April 2017; the preliminary results of the consultation were released on 31 May 2017 in the report: *Summary Report of the Public Consultation on Building a European Data Economy* (EC, 2017c).

Open science

Developing open science is one of the three main goals of the EU research and innovation policy, along with being open to innovation and open to the world:

Open Science represents a new approach to the scientific process based on cooperative work and new ways of diffusing knowledge by using digital technologies and new collaborative tools. The idea captures a systemic change to the way science and research have been carried out for the last fifty years: shifting from the standard practices of publishing research results in scientific publications towards sharing and using all available knowledge at an earlier stage in the research process. (DG RTD, 2016a)

A very effective (if informal) definition of 'open science' was given by Michael Nielsen on 28 July 2011 in the 'open science' discussion list, as follows:

Open science is the idea that scientific knowledge of all kinds should be openly shared as early as is practical in the discovery process.

By scientific knowledge 'of all kinds' I include journal articles, data, code, online software tools, questions, ideas, and speculations; anything which can be considered knowledge.

The 'as is practical' clause is included because very often there are other factors (legal, ethical, social, etc.) that must be considered.

This can get extremely complex, and requires, in my opinion, extended discussion. (Nielsen, 2011)

In order to reach a common conceptualisation and consensus about 'open science' the EC launched a public consultation between July and September 2014. See EC (2015) for results of the consultation, which lay the groundwork for the EC initiatives that follow one another from April 2016 onwards.

Since April 2016, in fact, a number of policy initiatives have been launched by the EC towards coupling the two goals of open access to publications and open data. More specifically, open research data acquired equal status to open publications, both converging and constituting the overall goal of open science.

Among the milestones of the EC policies is COM (2016) 0178: 'European Cloud Initiative: building a competitive data and knowledge economy in Europe' (EC, 2016), where both data and knowledge are emphasised and recognised as pivotal factors for the European economy.

These are some of the main questions it addressed:

How to maximise the incentives for sharing data and to increase the capacity to exploit them?
How to ensure that data can be used as widely as possible, across scientific disciplines and between the public and the private sector?
How better to interconnect the existing and the new data infrastructures across Europe?
How best to coordinate the support available to European data infrastructures as they move towards exascale computing?

In the 'Council Conclusions on the Transition Towards an Open Science System' released on 27 May 2016 the Council of the European Union formally stressed that 'open science entails among others open access to scientific publications and optimal reuse of research data'. A section of the document is devoted to optimal reuse of research data and in its last point emphasises the following:

the opportunities for the optimal reuse of research data can only be realised if data are consistent with the FAIR principles (findable, accessible, interoperable and re-usable) within a secure and trustworthy environment; RECALLS the importance of storage, long term preservation and curation of research data, taking into consideration the capacity of the research group or organisation, as well as ensuring the existence of metadata based on international standards; ENCOURAGES Member States, the Commission and stakeholders to follow the FAIR principles in research programmes and funding mechanisms.

(Council of the European Union, 2016)

In the EU policies for open science three main strands of action can be identified:

- the European Open Science Cloud: an infrastructural environment for open science, supporting the FAIR (findability, accessibility, interoperability and reusability) principles for research data
- the Open Science Policy Platform
- the Open Science Monitor.

The European Open Science Cloud (EOSC) Declaration (26 October 2017) set a number of priorities and actions for the implementation of the EOSC by 2020.

On October 2016, the High Level Expert Group European Open Science Cloud – established in 2015 – produced the report *Realising the European Open Science Cloud* (DG RTD, 2016b), within its mission to advise the Commission for the implementation of the EOSC. The report states:

The EOSC is a need emerging from science in transition. The EOSC is indeed European, but it should also be interoperable with the Internet of FAIR data and services and be an accessible infrastructure for modern research and innovation. It includes the required human expertise, resources, standards, best practices and underpinning infrastructures. It will have to support the Finding, Access, Interoperation and in particular the Re-use of open, as well as sensitive and properly secured data. It will also have to support the data related elements (software, standards, protocols, workflows) that enable re-use and data driven knowledge discovery and innovation.
KEY FACTORS FOR THE EFFECTIVE DEVELOPMENT OF THE EOSC AS PART OF OPEN SCIENCE
New modes of scholarly communication (with emphasis on machine actionability) need to be implemented.

Modern reward and recognition practices need to support data sharing and re-use.

Core data experts need to be trained and their career perspective significantly improved.

Innovative, fit for purpose funding schemes are needed to support sustainable underpinning infrastructures and core resources.

A real stimulus of multi-disciplinary collaboration requires specific measures in terms of review, funding and infrastructure.

The transition from scientific insights towards innovation needs a dedicated support policy.

The EOSC needs to be developed as a data infrastructure commons, that is an eco-system of infrastructures.

Where possible, the EOSC should enable automation of data processing and thus machine actionability is key.

Lightweight but internationally effective guiding governance should be developed.

Key performance indicators should be developed for the EOSC.

(DG RTD, 2016b)

On 21 June 2017, the Commission set up the new High Level Expert Group European Open Science Cloud 2017–2018, which runs from June 2017 to the end of 2018.

On 27 May 2016 the Directorate-General for Research and Innovation establishes the Commission High Level Advisory Group Open Science Policy Platform to provide advice about the development and implementation of open science policy in Europe.

A draft European open science agenda is available and provides a detailed framework of the various EC activities converging towards the open science strategy (RTD, 2016).

It is worth noting for the purpose of this publication that a group of experts – Horizon 2020 Commission Expert Group on Turning FAIR Data into Reality (E03464) – has been established with a mission to make FAIR data sharing the default for scientific research by 2020:

Findable, accessible, interoperable and re-usable/re-producible (FAIR) data is an integral part in the process of opening up science and research. By improving the FAIR-ness of research data it will unlock the potential for both scientific research and society to draw from the benefits of this data, and also enable significant contribution to economic growth. Accordingly, the Open Science agenda contains the ambition to make FAIR data sharing the default for scientific research by 2020. The overall objective of the Expert Group on Turning FAIR data into reality is to operationalise and facilitate this goal.

(FAIRdata, 2016)

An important concrete step towards achieving this goal is included in the Horizon 2020 Work Programme 2017, where the open research data pilot scope is extended to cover all thematic areas of Horizon 2020, so as to make open research data the default.

Research infrastructures

This is the definition of a research infrastructure in one of the regulatory documents of the European Union:

facilities, resources and related services that are used by the scientific community to conduct top-level research in their respective fields and covers major scientific equipment or sets of instruments; knowledge-based resources such as collections, archives or structures for scientific information; enabling Information and Communications Technology-based infrastructures such as Grid, computing, software and communication, or any other entity of a unique nature essential to achieve excellence in research.   (EC, 2009)

Such infrastructures may be 'single-sited' or 'distributed' (an organised network of resources) (EC, 2009). Research infrastructures constitute powerful tools enabling new data-intensive and collaborative research paradigms. They are operative tools conceived for international collaboration through a shared management of research resources. As distributed and shared resources, research infrastructures pose a series of problems as to the responsibility for the updating and maintenance of each infrastructure, besides the guarantee of financial sustainability for its long-term preservation. A legal answer to these problems is provided by the Community Legal Framework for a European Research Infrastructure Consortium (ERIC), initially issued in 2009, and regularly refined. In April 2010 the

Directorate-General for Research released the practical guidelines for the correct application for ERIC (DG Research, 2010).

In 2002 the European Strategy Forum on Research Infrastructures (ESFRI) was set up with the aim to 'support a coherent and strategy-led approach to policy-making on research infrastructures in Europe and to facilitate multilateral initiatives leading to the better use and development of research infrastructures', bringing together representatives from the EU member states, the associated states and a representative of the EC.

ESFRI maintains an observatory on research infrastructures in Europe and 'the ESFRI Roadmap identifies new research infrastructures of pan-European interest corresponding to the long term needs of the European research communities, covering all scientific areas, regardless of possible location' (ESFRI, 2011).

EU policies for knowledge transfer

In the EU recommendations on scientific information, the image of scientific research 'enslaved' to its applications, whether commercial or social, clearly remains in the background, while it is decidedly brought into the limelight in the EU recommendations on knowledge transfer. This is by no means surprising, since knowledge transfer is a process specifically aimed at communicating scientific results to enterprises, so that they can create usable products and services. Indeed, it is one of the channels used for the communication of scientific results, which, as mentioned elsewhere, occurs along three channels: within the scientific community ('scholarly communication'), between the scientific community and enterprises ('knowledge transfer'), and between the scientific community and society ('public understanding of science').

Hence, the EU view about the strategic role of knowledge transfer has been expressed in a series of official documents such as, just to mention a few: COM (2007) on Knowledge Transfer Between Research Institutions and Industry across Europe, followed by recommendation COM (2008) and by COM(2010). The latter communication promotes the concept of 'knowledge alliances' between education and business, which 'will help universities to modernise towards inter-disciplinarity, entrepreneurship and stronger business partnerships'.

From the point of view of information policies, it is worth noting that three items in the list of commitments made in connection with the Innovation Union objectives in COM(2010) 546 regard distinct information policy lines and effectively summarise EU expectations for what concerns scientific information and research behaviours:

- 20 open access to the results of publicly funded research activities
- 21 effective transfer of research results
- 22 development of a European knowledge market for patents and licensing.

Concluding remarks

Scientific information policies must be seen as an overarching concept, encompassing a range of diverse but tightly interconnected areas of policy. In this chapter an attempt has been made to outline these various dimensions and, mainly, the logic behind their development.

These and other matters are also among the research themes of the research project Information Policies in Science (IPS): Knowledge Sharing and Transfer in Scholarly Disciplines, co-ordinated by the Ceris Institute of the Italian National Research Council. Starting from two complex fields of investigation – scientific information policies and disciplinary studies – the IPS project concentrates on:

- characterising traditional and innovative information behaviour of humanities scholars and the ways in which research results are shared in the humanities, in literature, data and research infrastructures
- mapping and comparing scientific information policies in and for the European research area
- identifying feasibility requirements and best practices of the process of knowledge transfer in the humanities, including the potential involvement of different types of intermediary institutions (Consiglio Nazionale delle Ricerche, 2009).

The IPS project and this chapter assume there is awareness that policy measures for scientific information have been, and will continue to be, subject to periodic review and reformulation, depending on factors internal and external to the scientific system.

A second pillar of the analysis is the assumption that the processes of knowledge sharing and transfer are considered as crucial to support innovation and economic development.

References

Basili, C. (2009) Information Policies from the Republic of Science to the Realm of Innovation, in Pietruch-Reizes, D., Babik, W. and Frączek, R. (eds), *Safe, Innovational and Accessible Information: the perspectives for the information industry in the knowledge society*, Polish Society of Scientific Information, 30–48.

Basili, C. (2010) Politiche dell'informazione Scientifica tra Ricerca e Innovazione in Italia, in Basili, C. (ed.), *Sinergie Invisibili: ricerca e informazione scientifica nell'economia della conoscenza*, Cnr, 17–71.

Basili, C. (2013) Oltre la Comunicazione Scientifica: riflessioni sul trasferimento della conoscenza nelle scienze umane [Beyond Scholarly Communication: about knowledge transfer in the humanities], *AIB Studi*, **53** (2), 111–17.

Borgman, C. L. (2012) The Conundrum of Sharing Research Data, *Journal of the Association for Information Science and Technology*, **63**, 1059–78.

COM(2007) 182, Improving Knowledge Transfer Between Research Institutions and Industry across Europe: embracing open innovation – Implementing the Lisbon agenda, http://ec.europa.eu/invest-in-research/pdf/download_en/knowledge_transfe_07.pdf.

COM(2008) Commission Recommendation of 10 April 2008 on the management of intellectual property in knowledge transfer activities and Code of Practice for universities and other public research organisations, https://eur-lex.europa.eu/legal-content/EN/TXT/?uri=CELEX%3A32008H0416.

COM(2010) 'Europe 2020 Flagship Initiative – innovation union, https://ec.europa.eu/research/innovation-union/pdf/innovation-union-communication_en.pdf.

Consiglio Nazionale delle Ricerche (2009) *Information Policies in Science*, www.ceris.cnr.it/Basili/information_policies_in_science.htm.

Council of the European Union (2016) Council Conclusions on the Transition Towards an Open Science System, adopted by the Council at

its 3470th meeting held on 27 May, No. 9526/16,
http://data.consilium.europa.eu/doc/document/ST-9526-2016-INIT/
en/pdf.

Cragin, M. H., Palmer, C. L., Carlson, J. R. and Witt, M. (2010) Data Sharing,
Small Science and Institutional Repositories, *Philosophical Transactions of
the Royal Society A: Mathematical, Physical and Engineering Sciences*, **368**
(1926), 4023–38.

David, P. A. and Foray, D. (2002) An Introduction to the Economy of the
Knowledge Society, *International Social Science Journal*, **54** (171), 9–23.

DG Research (2010) *Legal Framework for a European Research Infrastructure
Consortium: ERIC, practical guidelines*, Directorate-General for Research,
http://ec.europa.eu/research/infrastructures/pdf/eric_en.pdf.

DG RTD (2016a) *Open Innovation, Open Science, Open to the World: a vision for
Europe*, European Commission Directorate-General for Research and
Innovation, doi: 10.2777/061652.

DG RTD (2016b) *Realising the European Open Science Cloud: first report and
recommendations of the Commission High Level Expert Group on the European
Open Science Cloud*, European Commission Directorate-General for
Research and Innovation, doi: 10.2777/940154.

EC (1999) eEurope: an information society for all, communication on a
Commission initiative for the special European Council of Lisbon, 23 and
24 March 2000, COM/99/0687 final, European Commission.

EC (2000) Towards a European Research Area, COM/2000/6, European
Commission.

EC (2006a) *Study on the Economic and Technical Evolution of the Scientific
Publication Markets in Europe*, European Commission,
http://europa.eu/rapid/press-release_IP-06-414_en.htm.

EC (2006b) Summary of the Responses to the Public Consultation on the
'Study on the Economic and Technical Evolution of the Scientific
Publication Markets in Europe' commissioned by the Research
Directorate-General (Directorate L – Science, economy and society),
European Commission.

EC (2007) *Scientific Information in the Digital Age: access, dissemination and
preservation*, Communication from the Commission to the Council, the
European Parliament, the Economic and Social Committee and the
Committee of the Regions, COM/2007/56 final, European Commission.

EC (2009) *Community Legal Framework for a European Research Infrastructure
Consortium (ERIC)*, Council Regulation (EC) No. 723/2009, European

Commission.

EC (2011a) *Open Data: an engine for innovation, growth and transparent governance*, COM(2011) 882 final, European Commission.

EC (2011b) STI Consultation on Scientific Information in the Digital Age, https://ec.europa.eu/research/consultations/scientific_information/ consultation_en.htm.

EC (2012a) A Reinforced European Research Area Partnership for Excellence and Growth, COM/2012/392, European Commission.

EC (2012b) Recommendation on Access to and Preservation of Scientific Information, C/2012/4890, European Commission.

EC (2012c) Towards Better Access to Scientific Information: boosting the benefits of public investments in research, COM/2012/401, European Commission.

EC (2013) *Public Consultation on Open Research Data*, European Commission, http://ec.europa.eu/research/science-society/document_library/pdf_06/ report_2013-07-open_research_data-consultation.pdf.

EC (2015) *Validation of the Results of the Public Consultation on Science 2.0: science in transition*, European Commission, www.eesc.europa.eu/resources/docs/validation-of-the-results-of-the- public-consultation-on-science-20.pdf.

EC (2016) *European Cloud Initiative: building a competitive data and knowledge economy in Europe*, COM/2016/0178 final, European Commission.

EC (2017a) *Building a European Data Economy*, COM/2017/9 final, European Commission.

EC (2017b) Staff Working Document on the Free Flow of Data and Emerging Issues of the European Data Economy Accompanying the Document Communication 'Building a European Data Economy' {COM(2017) 9 final}.

EC (2017c) *Summary Report of the Public Consultation on Building a European Data Economy*, European Commission, https://ec.europa.eu/digital-single- market/en/news/summary-report-public-consultation-building-european -data-economy.

EESC (2012) Opinion of the European Economic and Social Committee on 'Towards Better Access to Scientific Information: boosting the benefits of public investments in research', COM/2012/401 final (2013/C 76/09), European Economic and Social Committee.

EP (2006) Decision No. 1982/2006/EC of the European Parliament and of the Council of 18 December concerning the Seventh Framework Programme of the European Community for Research, Technological Development and Demonstration Activities (2007–2013), European Parliament.

ESFRI (2011) *Strategy Report on Research Infrastructures: Roadmap 2010*, European Strategy Forum on Research Infrastructures, http://ec.europa.eu/research/infrastructures/pdf/esfri-strategy_ report_and_roadmap.pdf.

Etzkowitz, H. and Leydesdorff, L. (1998) The Endless Transition: a 'triple helix' of university-industry-government relations, *Minerva*, **36**, 203–8.

FAIRdata (2016). Horizon 2020 Commission expert group on Turning FAIR data into reality (E03464), http://ec.europa.eu/transparency/regexpert/index.cfm?do= groupDetail.groupDetail&groupID=3464.

Gibbons, M., Limoges, C., Nowotny, H., Schwartzman, S., Scott, P. and Trow, M. (1994) *The New Production of Knowledge: the dynamics of science and research in contemporary societies*, Sage.

Godin, B. (2008) *The Information Economy: the history of a concept through its measurement, 1949–2005*, Project on History and Sociology of S&T Statistics, Working Paper 38.

Hjørland, B., Søndergaard, T. F. and Andersen, J. (2003) Documents and the Communication of Scientific and Scholarly Information: revising and updating the UNISIST model, *Journal of Documentation*, **59** (3), 278–320.

IFAP (2007) Information for All Programme. (Revised) Draft Strategic Plan (2008–2013), UNESCO, www.ifapcom.ru/files/Documents/ifap_draf_strategic_plan.pdf.

Merton, R. K. (1942) The Normative Structure of Science, in Storer, N. W. (ed.), *The Sociology of Science: theoretical and empirical investigations*, University of Chicago Press, 1973, 267–78.

National Research Council (1959) *Proceedings of the International Conference on Scientific Information*, The National Academies Press.

Nielsen, M. (2011) Definitions of Open Science? Email message, https://lists.okfn.org/pipermail/open-science/2011-July/000907.html.

OECD (1962) The Function of OECD in the Field of Scientific and Technical Information, SR(62)25, Organisation for Economic Co-operation and Development, as cited by Godin (2008).

OECD (2007) *Principles and Guidelines for Access to Research Data from Public Funding*, Organisation for Economic Co-operation and Development.

RTD (2016) Directorate General for Research and Innovation (RTD). Draft European Open Science Agenda, https://ec.europa.eu/research/openscience/pdf/draft_european_ open_science_agenda.pdf#view=fit&pagemode=none (last updates at the time of writing from 2016).

Sörlin, S. and Vessuri, H. (2007) *Knowledge Society vs Knowledge Economy: knowledge, power, and politics*, Palgrave McMillan.

UNESCO (1979) Intergovernmental Council for the General Information Programme, final report, 2nd session, PGI.79/CONF.202/COL.13; PGI/COUNCIL/II/5, UNESCO.

UNESCO (1988) *Review of the General Information Programme 1977–1987: a compilation of information on its characteristics, activities and accomplishments*, PGI.88/WS/19, UNESCO.

Webster, F. (2006) *Theories of the Information Society*, 3rd edn, Routledge, Taylor & Francis.

Wood, J., Andersson, T., Bachem, A., Best, C., Genova, F., Lopez, D. R. and Hudson, R. L. (2010) *Riding the Wave: how Europe can gain from the rising tide of scientific data*, final report of the High Level Expert Group on Scientific Data.

Ziman, J. M. (1995) *Of One Mind: the collectivization of science*, American Institute of Physics.

6

Access to digital archives: studying users' expectations and behaviours

Pierluigi Feliciati

Archivists have traditionally dedicated little time and attention to studying their users; archivists focus, first and foremost, on the care and preservation of records, and only secondarily on records' use.

(Duff, 2012, 199)

Users, archivists and their interaction

Almost 20 years ago the famous Canadian archivist Barbara Craig gave the title 'Old Myths in New Clothes: expectations of archives users' to her contribution to a conference on archives' public (Craig, 1998). She provided evidence that there is a risk that archives are 'condemned by their own methods to fall short in meeting the needs of their users'; she also argued that this is not a new issue, but 'an updated version of the familiar scenario in which it is assumed that conflicting demands and distinctions exist between select services for an élite clientele and popular appeal and services for the many'. The popular myth that the world wide web contains every possible information enforces the misconceptions about the nature of users and their access behaviours, so 'it is crucial that the energy behind our concern not dissipate in complaining', but archivists should accept that 'the many varieties of myth surrounding information technology contain a core of reality for users and for archives'.

Users follow different strategies

The development of digital environments for offering access to archival information requires considering different scenarios of use. The popular typology of internet users includes two categories – browsers (or surfers) and searchers, where the browser typically follows multiple links mostly for amusement, and the searcher is seeking specific information. Actually back in 1977 when discussing the wider case of information retrieval, Carl Beck introduced three categories, browsers, searchers and reductionists (Beck, 1977).

Carl Beck summarised their strategies and we are providing his description here because it is insightful about not only users' interactions with digital material, but also the long way digital collections have developed over 40 years.

A *browser* is typically a person who wants to be brought up to date on some specific field or subfield. Browsers are interested in all the information that meet their criteria. They are not particularly concerned with the preciseness of the fit of the material retrieved to their search strategy. They tend to evaluate a system on its comprehensiveness and judge a system on its ability to recall.

Searchers for specific information are interested in an exact fit between their information needs, specifications and the output they receive. They evaluate the system by the exactness of the fit of the information retrieved to the specifications agreed on. The searcher for specifics judges a system on its ability to be precise.

The *reductionist* is concerned about the interrelationships between various sets of information. Persons analysing content or trying to map images or perceptions, and who use such information to analyse behaviour, fall into this category. The reductionist is interested not only in the object under discussion, but also the actor's orientation towards that object, the perception that the actor has of that object, and the intentions of the actor. The reductionist is concerned with such linguistic dimensions as negative–positive, weak–strong and active–inactive.

Reductionists are often interested in developing cognitive maps and then applying mathematical models or graph theory to their findings. They find that no information retrieval system or service is designed that automatically meet their needs and so they usually rely on self-generated codebooks or dictionaries.

Although this third role, the reductionist, had been abandoned from the popular dichotomy of users, it actually captures characteristics which are very relevant to the use of specialised digital collections and archival materials. Powered lately with semantic web and novel information visualisations, we are still working to resolve issues which were formulated almost half a century ago.

Let us highlight how the two popular roles, of the browser and searcher, are modified within the digital archives context.

The 'browsing attitude' implies the informed adoption of the advanced search strategies typical of the so-called 'berry picking' behaviour. Archival browsers have a research plan, verify their theories on documents, and are good finding aids readers, knowledgeable in the archives' life cycle. They include and exclude different search paths, and could appreciate the lack of records as useful information and consider serendipity as a value. They know that archival research needs time.

Second, the 'searching attitude' – the seeking of single units of information, without any attention to context – is based on looking for specific data. This approach does not start from theories, it insists on quick results and is not open to decode complex finding aids, preferring miraculous fishing tools. But it is not acceptable to create digital resources and infrastructures which match only the first profile, experienced in browsing the traditional structure of archival description, and to consider 'newbies' or users who search for quick answers to specific questions as a problem.

These different user demands illustrate that there is an evident problem in delivering archival information in context, on site or online: the necessity of contextualisation (both logical, in what file or series do the records reside, and historical, who were the creators and what activities motivated the creation of the records) marks an important difference with libraries and museums. Archival information is not only made of description of records, but includes interpretations and reproductions. The golden rule of archival description suggests providing information about records, their current location, their creators and historical context and about the available finding aids, plus their necessary, qualified relations. Archivists are traditionally expected to play a mediation role even when visitors want to use finding aids. This 'extended mediation' implies that archives reveal themselves gradually, to a predetermined audience, passing through archivists' intermediation (Figure 6.1).

> Finding aid is the 'broadest term to cover any description or means of reference made or received by an archives service in the course of establishing administrative or intellectual control over archival material' (ICA, 2000, Glossary).

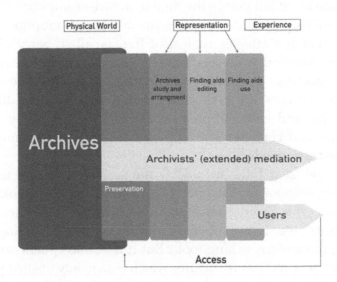

Figure 6.1 *The traditional extended mediation of archivists (Feliciati and Alfier, 2013b, 102)*

Archival descriptions meeting the users

In the last decade of the 20th century, the International Council of Archives (ICA) defined a set of internationally shared standards and guidelines, highlighting the requirement for a reduction of archival mediation in the finding aids editing cycle. The adoption of the International Standard for Archival Description (ICA, 2000, I.5) 'is part of a process that will ensure the creation of consistent, appropriate, and self-explanatory descriptions'. The Guidelines for the Preparation and Presentation of Finding Aids clarified that 'the principles which govern the preparation of finding aids are: a) to provide access to archival material by communicating information about them to users; b) to produce accurate, consistent and self-explanatory finding aids' (International Council on Archives, 2001, 2.2). Recently, the need for archival information to reduce its cognitive distance from users was confirmed in the ICA Principles of Access to Archives: '[archivists] are continually alert to changing technologies of communication and use those that are available and practical to promote the knowledge of archives. Archivists consider user needs when determining how the archives are published' (ICA, 2012, 3). The ICA standards insist that access resources should tend to convey information to users in more direct ways, emancipated by the traditional 'negotiation' of archivists in reference rooms, and assuming that not all research questions could be forecasted (Yakel, 2003, 192).

Recently, a draft of a new conceptual model was released by the ICA Experts Group on Archival Description, Records in Contexts (ICA and EGAD, 2016), to integrate the four descriptive standards. The new standard tries to answer the challenges of the present technological landscape, going over the traditional production of multilevel and connected descriptions in favour of multidimensional nets of information resources, in the form of Resource Description Framework statements. This tendency to multi-contextualise the archival pieces of information surely opens up new possibilities of cross-sector interoperability and openness to semantic web opportunities. At the same time, though, it is hard to foresee if this Copernican revolution would give more attention to final users, both in content usability and by involving them proactively, even in testing activities.

In short, the traditional model had to come to grips with the massive offer of innovative tools and web services. The increased access to archives does not imply automatically there is a parallel increase of accessibility and quality in accessing and using archival information. On the contrary, on the web the mediation role played by archivists in reference rooms is highlighted, due to the peculiar characteristics of the hypertext model: interactivity (freedom to act on information), multi-sequentiality (non-linear use of information), association (freedom to compose information), itinerary (access to information based on the navigating), process (information as a dynamic phenomenon in which there are no discontinuities) and openness (non-hierarchical and distributed production of information) (Fiormonte, 2003, 83–84). Can we really accept that traditional archival information is safe from the remarkable set of changes affecting all the analogue texts produced by our traditional printing culture? To what extent are archival finding aids ready to be published on the web, where users are called to act as protagonists of the cognitive process, basically free from any mediation?

The need for a paradigm shift in digital archives

To respond to the challenge of answering user's needs in a more user-centric manner, Wendy Scheir highlighted correctly that 'it is essential to establish clear distinction between input and output, even while acknowledging that description and presentation are inextricably intertwined' (2006, 50–51). Many archivists do not agree with the principle that 'output is not input': their common assumption is that compliance with methodological and data structure standards is not just necessary but sufficient to guarantee a good transmission of primary sources to web users, as if such standards had an extensive force in supporting both input and output. In other words, the historical-technicist model emphasises standardisation in a reductive way, with a hidden bias against the accurate presentation of archives (Ribeiro, 2001). An effective archival mediation, especially in digital environments, depends on achieving a clear distinction between input standards, controlling the increasingly sophisticated archival descriptive techniques, and output models that could guide the development of the best displays for end-users.

If we take into account some of the factors that typically reduce the usability of archival data on the web, for example the 'inter-indexer inconsistency' or the issues in retrieving archival descriptions from general search engines, the need for a shared reference model, similar to those available for the neighbouring sector of digital libraries, becomes evident (Feliciati and Alfier, 2014). The goal is to overcome the traditional approach to finding aids and provide new, online aids that meet all users' needs'. A 'secular approach' asks for dynamic environments, where the core content is represented by information created and managed by archivists, which can be enriched and reinterpreted with the participation of the users. In other words, it has to be legitimised in a 'shared authority' model (Duff and Harris, 2002) even for archival descriptions, opening the transformation of finding aids into 'information social phenomena' (Ribeiro, 2001) (Figure 6.2 opposite).

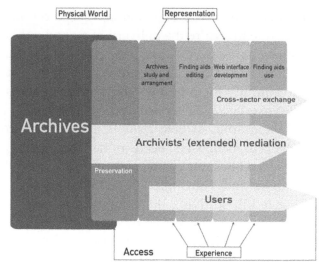

Figure 6.2 *A shared authority mediation model (Feliciati and Alfier, 2013b, 107)*

Just to start the process, archives online should embed tools which are able to replace human mediation, such as virtual reference, recommender and reputation systems, visitor awareness services, and user generated content services like social tagging, social bookmarking, folksonomies, wikis, commenting and notations (Yakel, 2003).

In this altered framework, it is crucial to consider also the 'interfering' action of a new, powerful subject, unknown in the analogue world: the user agent. More and more often users have access to digital finding aids not directly, but through the mediation of automatic tools: robots, spiders, crawlers, harvesters and so on (Nicholas and Clark, 2012). Their influence on users demonstrates the 'hidden collections phenomenon': archival information systems in their present shape are useless, invisible to users, if their content is not indexed correctly by general search engines (Schaffner, 2009).

To conclude, finding aids for online access resources should be based on what users need, in order to increase their quality and appropriateness, so users can achieve their goals effectively, productively, safely and efficiently (ISO/IEC, 2001; Kitchenham and Pfleeger, 1996).

Ask the archival users

Within this renewed paradigm of archival mediation, the activities devoted to understanding needs, expectations and perceptions of users assume a crucial role to ensure the delivery of a good online archival service. User studies are essential to check that finding aids are self-explanatory and usable. The goal should not be to trivialise digital archives, but to simplify them to meet users' requirements. Michael Cook warned 25 years ago against meeting 'every customer profile and every market demographic' (Cook, 1990/91, 127), hoping conversely that archivists have to meet users' needs rather than users' wants.

Research areas about information behaviour (Wilson, 1999) and user experience (Mahlke and Thüring, 2007) are the starting point for archivists interested in studying their users, at least because these approaches are strongly characterised by acknowledging the value of empirical research. Another contribution comes directly from marketing, through audience measurement, classifying users on the basis of their possible quality as consumers. They are not treated individually, but gathered into consumer market segments, groups of people with a similar perception of a requirement, its characteristics and motivations, demonstrating an homogeneous behaviour in solving a particular problem. The typical methods of this approach are based on collecting indirect data (mostly log analysis of web servers) and direct data (with some involvement of real users), typically quantitative.

The studies on archives online to check users' satisfaction, involving people external to development staff, could be even more useful during the early stages of a project. Any evaluation is called formative if it is conducted while the digital platform is still under development; some data gathered during this stage focuses on content and functionalities and how these correspond to users' needs (Tsakonas, 2012). Those needs could be checked by asking users directly, collecting precious feedback to help address flaws in the interaction design. Moreover, experts can provide precious assistance as soon as the prototype has been refined, giving their insights into the quality features of the system. Figure 6.3 (opposite) shows a time line of design and evaluation of digital libraries.

To involve users directly in the prototype step, it could be useful to launch a survey (e.g. using questionnaires), but this method is only suitable if there is a coherent community to complete it. A more complex and useful method is to organise one or more moderated

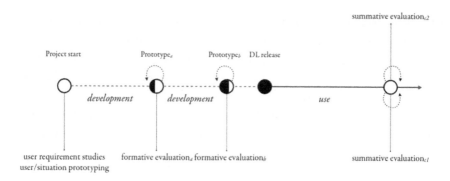

Figure 6.3 *A time line of design and evaluation of digital libraries [Tsakonas, 2012, Figure 5.1]*

focus groups, asking a panel of significant participants to complete specific tasks using the access platform and then analyse their results.

'Probably one of the most confusing elements of user studies is that there is no clear allocation of types of studies for a particular purpose and the same methods can be used on different stages of the Digital Library development' (Dobreva, O'Dwyer and Feliciati, 2012, 249). Some handbooks and guidelines are available for this purpose, but before choosing which method of user study to use (web question-naire, focus groups, expert evaluation, deep log analysis, interviews, etc.), those interested should start by considering what roles users are supposed to play: what type of user involvement is suitable to answer different user-related research questions.

In the last decade the effectiveness of online archival information started to be tested, mostly in North America and more recently in Europe (Duff, 2012). Drawing on the most relevant surveys of users of archives (Agosti et al., 2013; Chapman, 2010; Daniels and Yakel, 2010; Duff and Stoyanova, 1998; Feliciati, 2012; Feliciati and Alfier 2013a, 2013b; Scheir, 2006; Yakel, 2004) and the most significant studies in the digital library domain (Dobreva et al., 2010a, 2010b), it is possible to consider the needs of archive users, despite the variety of measuring techniques and the different resources analysed.

These studies have not been consolidated into a common evaluation framework and usually demonstrate how research on users' interaction behaviour with archival information online still needs to be deepened and broadened. By sharing methodologies and results it is possible to build a more complete, normalised and comparative research framework. The first issue to be noticed about most of the studies is that each research study has applied its own protocol, tailored to the characteristics of the digital environment to be evaluated and special settings. This hinders significantly the opportunity to compare data from different surveys, with a historic series of data, so it would be very useful to compile and share a classification of the typical expected features of archives online, to structure studies on and to analyse on a large scale how changes of archival displays may affect how they are used.

The second issue regards the frequent small size of panels involved, reducing the relevance and reliability of the data collected. Panels were typically selected from groups of the population interested in online finding aids, for example young people, scholars (Duff, 2012, 200), or people coming from the same geographical and cultural context as the primary sources described by finding aids. A shared classification of digital archive users' profiles, or a portfolio of usage scenarios or personas (Rasmussen and Petersen, 2012), could be helpful when designing new research methods and comparing their results. Some studies were conducted without distinguishing between novice archival researchers and advanced scholars, a relevant issue if we consider that these two groups have very varied strategies of interaction with archival information, and so it is wise to organise two clearly distinct sub-panels within the same survey. Those undertaking studies should verify the ICT background of participants who take part in demographic questionnaires on archives, and interpret the results with this in mind.

A *usage scenario* is 'a real-world example of how one or more people or organisations interact with a system, detailing the steps, events and actions which occur during the interaction. Usage scenarios can be very detailed or reasonably high level describing critical actions but not then indicating how they're performed.'

A *persona* is 'a fictional character with all the characteristics of the user'. Personas often include an image and a name and typically include demographic information such as age, gender, occupation and income. Personas carry other information, such as user goals, concerns, motivations and expectations (Dobreva, O'Dwyer and Feliciati, 2012, Glossary).

Analysis of the principal surveys of archival displays listed above showed there were four main concerns among online users of archives:

- archival terminology
- the hierarchical structure of descriptions
- searching tools
- content visualisation.

All the studies concur that the language used within online archival finding aids is often too technical and represents a barrier for users. Even basic archival terms (like funds) are not immediately understandable. The barriers generated by archival jargon condition not only the comprehension of descriptions, but also the use of the extended search functions, as most users do not understand them and therefore cannot use them, since they are typically based on complex and ambiguous labels deduced from archival language. Other barriers arise because archivists usually populate their description with historical terms appearing on primary sources or traditionally used for archival description, which are not necessarily predictable by final users.

It was widely noticed that users had difficulty in moving through the multilevel hierarchies typical of archival descriptions, although some inexperienced users demonstrated an unexpected ability to learn the structured nature of archival resources. The ambiguity of the hierarchy of archives leads users to prefer search functions to retrieve information rather than browse through descriptive levels as they find what they are looking for more quickly using that method. If the users are interested in what archives are related to (in the 'aboutness', in content datum), archivists concentrate on what archives are composed of, the internal relations among descriptive items, and the structural datum, following strictly the principle that archival records are not records about an activity, but records of an activity. The issues related to hierarchical structures seem to be more evident for users with little or no direct experience of archival research. Some research results suggest that users tend to think there are no logical criteria guiding the structure of archives – as there are, actually – but that they are organised according to their material characteristics. The surveys sometimes had inconsistent results about the importance or not of the hierarchical structure of archives. Some studies gathered clear evidence that the multilevel structure is not difficult in itself for users to understand, but that understanding depends mostly on the clarity of displays.

The user studies showed the critical importance of the search functionalities that are typically implemented within browsing across different levels of hierarchical descriptions. Users were accustomed to online public access catalogues and item-based digital libraries, and tended to think that query methods are identical for archival finding aids and bibliographical catalogues. They seem to have difficulty in choosing terms or search parameters, as they are too complex. They often prefer to adopt the default values proposed by the systems. This inability precludes any refining of results. Other critical factors arise from the presentation of search results: archivists traditionally have a non-evaluative attitude towards information, and tend to build up information systems neutrally, for example ordering lists alphabetically or chronologically. Archive users, on the contrary, are accustomed to general web search engines, and expect search results to be presented according to a semantic relevance rank (such as Google seems to do). The use of controlled dictionaries in subject-based queries was examined, but without conclusive results as surveys did not demonstrate that users carried out subject-based queries coherently. Some studies found that users appreciate using authority records for keywords (access keys), because of their preference for knowing the 'aboutness' of archives, as explained above. Other studies presented a limited use of controlled dictionaries, perhaps because there was misunderstanding of the purpose of access keys and their connections with archival descriptions.

The studies carried out so far do not provide any unequivocal position on the content and use of archives. There are some contradictory signs relating to users' common preference for minimal descriptions rather than detailed and analytical ones. Some users appreciated using displays that presented short narrative texts linked to more detailed information, the popular 'see more' function.

Conclusion

This chapter demonstrated and argued that the goal of building up a reference model for archives online, including user studies, has to be shared with a wide community, made up of archivists and digital curators but open to digital librarians and information experts. To draft such a model, it is useful to focus mostly on shared characteristics and functions, instead of (existing) differences with the digital library domain, as discussed in Feliciati and Alfier (2013b; 2014).

Archival communities still have to accept that web environments undermine the traditional mediation role between archivists and users, first because they distinguish between web output and encoded input. This re-thinking calls for the contribution of cognitive science, human–computer interaction, web design and other application models, and above all should be based on the 'users' voices', as identified after carrying out appropriate user studies; Elaine Toms is one of the vocal information professionals who insists on the importance of understanding users' needs, expectations and information skills (2012).

The 21st century archivists are asked to build user centric displays, matching their descriptive techniques and standards with the study of software agents and real users, and checking the prototypes of archival web environments by applying appropriate evaluation and testing activities. Analysing the results of user studies is crucial when finalising the online platforms of archives in order to ensure they provide access of the best quality.

References

Agosti, M., Manfioletti, M., Orio, N., Ponchia, C. and Silvello, G. (2013) The Evaluation Approach of IPSA@CULTURA, presentation at the 9th Italian Research Conference on Digital Libraries,
www.dis.uniroma1.it/~ircdl13/?q=node/43.

Beck, C. (1977) Information Systems and Social Sciences, *American Behavioral Scientist*, **20** (3), 427–48.

Chapman, J. C. (2010) Observing Users: an empirical analysis of user interaction with online finding aids, *Journal of Archival Organization*, **8**, 4–30.

Cook, T. (1990/91) Viewing the World Upside Down: reflections on the theoretical underpinning of archival public programming, *Archivaria*, **31** (Winter), 123–34.

Craig, B. L. (1998) Old Myths in New Clothes: expectations of archives users, *Archivaria*, **45** (Spring), 118–26.

Daniels, M. G. and Yakel, E. (2010) Seek and You May Find: successful search in online finding aid systems, *American Archivist*, **73**, 535–68.

Dobreva, M., McCulloch, E., Birrell, D., Feliciati, P., Ruthven, I., Sykes, J. and Ünal, Y. (2010a) *User and Functional Testing: final report*, http://www.bby.hacettepe.edu.tr/e-bulten/dosyalar/file/unal-europeana.pdf.

Dobreva, M., Mcculloch, E., Birrell, D., Feliciati, P., Ruthven, I., Sykes, J. and Ünal, Y. (2010b) Digital Natives and Specialised Digital Libraries: a study of Europeana users, in Kurbanoglu, S. et al. (eds), *Technological Convergence and Social Networks in Information Management*, Springer-Verlag, 45–60.

Dobreva, M., O'Dwyer, A. and Feliciati, P. (eds) (2012) *User Studies for Digital Library Development*, Facet Publishing.

Duff, W. (2012) User Studies in Archives, in Dobreva, M., O'Dwyer, A. and Feliciati, P. (eds), *User Studies for Digital Library Development*, Facet Publishing, 199–206.

Duff, W. and Harris, V.(2002) Stories and Names: archival description as narrating records and constructing meanings, *Archival Science*, **2**, 263–85.

Duff, W. and Stoyanova, P. (1998) Transforming the Crazy Quilt: archival displays from user's point of view, *Archivaria*, **45**, 44–79.

Feliciati, P. (2012) Ask the Users, il valore aggiunto della valutazione dei sistemi informativi culturali on line coinvolgendo gli utenti: il caso del progetto 'Una Città per gli Archivi', *Il Capitale Culturale* [*Studies on the Value of Cultural Heritage*], May, 129–44, http://riviste.unimc.it/index.php/cap-cult/article/view/483.

Feliciati, P. and Alfier, A. (2013a) Archives on the Web and Users Expectations: towards a convergence with digital libraries, *Review of the National Center for Digitization*, **22**, 81–92, http://elib.mi.sanu.ac.rs/files/journals/ncd/22/ncd22081.pdf.

Feliciati, P. and Alfier, A. (2013b) Archives Online from Simple Access to Full Use: towards the development of a user-centered quality model?, *Archivi & Computer*, February, 98–112.

Feliciati, P. and Alfier, A. (2014) From Access to Use: premises for a user-tested quality model for the development of archives online, in Bolikowski, L., Casarosa, V. and Goodale, P. (eds), *Theory and Practice of Digital Libraries: TPDL 2013 selected workshops*, Communications in Computer and Information Science 416; Springer International Publishing, 174–9.

Fiormonte, D. (2003) *Scrittura e Filologia nell'era Digitale*, Bollati Boringhieri.

ICA (2000) *ISAD (G): general international standard archival description*, 2nd edn, International Council on Archives, www.ica.org/10207/standards/isadg-general-international-standard-archival-description-second-edition.html.

ICA (2001) *Guidelines for the Preparation and Presentation of Finding Aids*, International Council on Archives, www.icacds.org.uk/eng/findingaids.htm.

ICA (2012) *Principles of Access to Archives*, International Council on Archives, https://www.ica.org/sites/default/files/ICA_Access-principles_EN.pdf.

ICA and EGAD (2016) *Records in Contexts: a conceptual model for archival description*, consultation draft, International Council on Archives and Expert Group on Archival Description, September, www.ica.org/en/egad-ric-conceptual-model.

ISO/IEC 9126-1:2001, *Software Engineering – Product Quality – Part 1: Quality Model*, International Standards Organization.

Kitchenham, B. and Pfleeger, S. (1996) Software Quality: the elusive target, *IEEE Software*, **13** (1), 12–21.

Mahlke, S. and Thüring, M. (2007) Studying Antecedents of Emotional Experiences in Interactive Contexts, in *Proceedings of Computer/Human Interaction 2007 Conference*, ACM Press, 915–18.

Nicholas, D. and Clark, D. (2012) Evidence of User Behaviour: deep log analysis, in Dobreva, M., O'Dwyer, A. and Feliciati, P. (eds), *User Studies for Digital Library Development*, Facet Publishing, 85–94.

Rasmussen, K. G. and Petersen, G. (2012) Personas, in Dobreva, M., O'Dwyer, A. and Feliciati, P. (eds), *User Studies for Digital Library Development*, Facet Publishing, 105–13.

Ribeiro, F. (2001) Archival Science and Changes in the Paradigm, *Archival Science*, **1**, 295–310.

Schaffner, J. (2009) *The Metadata Is the Interface: better description for better discovery of archives and special collections, synthesized from user studies*, OCLC Research, www.oclc.org/content/dam/research/publications/library/2009/2009-06.pdf.

Scheir, W. (2006) First Entry: report on a qualitative exploratory study of novice user experience with online finding aids, *Journal of Archival Organization*, **3**, 49–85.

Toms, E.G. (2012) Models that Inform Digital Library Design, in Dobreva, M., O'Dwyer, A. and Feliciati, P. (eds), *User Studies for Digital Library*

Development, Facet Publishing, 21–32.

Tsakonas, G. (2012) Users within the Evaluation of Digital Libraries, in Dobreva, M., O'Dwyer, A. and Feliciati, P. (eds), *User Studies for Digital Library Development*, Facet Publishing, 51–61.

Wilson, T. D. (1999) Models in Information Behaviour Research, *Journal of Documentation*, **55** (3), 249–70.

Yakel, E. (2003) Impact of Internet-Based Discovery Tools on Use and Users of Archives, *Comma*, 191–200.

Yakel, E. (2004) Encoded Archival Description: are finding aids boundary spanners or barriers for users?, *Journal of Archival Organization*, **2**, 63–77.

Case studies

7

Research data archives: current data management and data audit practices

Elli Papadopoulou, Panayiota Polydoratou,
Sotirios Sismanis and Donald Tabone

Introduction

In the last decades, archives have been developed in order to preserve organisational and institutional research related outputs. These platforms today accommodate storage and preservation needs of discipline-specific research artefacts such as GenBank or The Archaeology Data Service, but also more generic ones, like figshare and Zenodo. In order to maximise their visibility and searchability, registries like re3data have been deployed to index them. Another form of platform ensuring long-term preservation are institutional repositories. These are multi-purpose academic infrastructures that were primarily developed to support the need to deposit institutional research outputs and records of academic and administrative activities. In the open access world, these serve the scope of green open access (open access to research publications implemented via deposit of publications to institutional repositories), which supports research archiving. However, in consequence of the research data management and data-intensive science flow prevailing in recent years, institutional repositories' content and capabilities have been extended and enhanced. The institutional repositories of the University of Pittsburgh, D-Scholarship @ Pitt, and the University of Cambridge, Apollo, form prime examples of such behaviour.

Research data archives are important to a number of user stakeholders:

- Archivists guide researchers and scholars when creating research data management plans; they ensure the longevity and potential re-use of data afterwards; they provide data anonymously when confidentiality is required; and tell researchers how long data will be preserved.
- General users seek datasets that have been properly described with metadata and thus are understandable; they require easy access to them.
- Funders promote data sharing and re-use, which enables cross discipline collaboration, makes research outputs cost-effective, and makes sharing of quality data more efficient while at the same time reducing the costs of conducting research.

The role of library and information scientists and computer scientists in setting up and managing research data archives is important. Scholars, being dedicated to the research process, are often unprepared for a number of risks that might occur such as natural disasters, facility infrastructure failure, storage failure, server hardware or software failure, application software failure, format obsolescence, legal encumbrance, human error, malicious attack, loss of staff competency, loss of institutional commitment, and loss of financial stability. Data sharing opens ways to better research by reducing the risk of scholars being accused of fraud; it can reduce the risk of duplicating research and collecting irrelevant data, and promote interdisciplinarity.

Hence, infrastructures which have a mission to support data life-cycle activities should be carefully chosen for researchers' data sharing, provided that they have previously been assessed to ensure they follow the correct practices when preserving data for perpetuity. The CoreTrustSeal certification (formerly Data Seal of Approval) provides guidelines for repositories (Data Seal of Approval, 2015).

Definitions and current trends

Before proceeding with an overview of current data management policies and data audit tools and practices, we define here the terms we use throughout this chapter:

- *Data archives*: These are scholarly services such as the National

Institute of Mental Health (NIMH) Data Archive (https://data-archive.nimh.nih.gov/), UK Data Archive, arXiv, which host and provide access to research data. For example, the National Institute of Mental Health Data Archive (NDA) is a digital archive, which offers a great variety of data gathered from several scientific fields. It delivers a framework in which data, tools and methods can become shareable and help build a strong relationship between science and discovery. Similarly, the UK Data Archive offers access to different types of data and is responsible for collecting and curating that data as well (UK Data Archive, 2018).

- *Data assets*: Data assets are data generated in the context of education, an academic career and during procedures that are financially supported (HATII, 2009, 6).
- *Data audit*: 'A data audit refers to the auditing of data to assess its quality or utility for a specific purpose. Auditing data, unlike auditing finances, involves looking at key metrics, other than quantity, to create conclusions about the properties of a data set' (Techopedia, 2018).
- *Data management plan*: Data management plans are those involved in the collection, organisation, management, storage, security, back-up, maintenance and sharing of data. They must address the dangers associated with data relating to re-use, sharing and storage. Strong data management plans often follow specific guidelines (University of Sheffield, 2018).
- *Data management planning*: Writing a data management plan involves defining numerous matters clearly. A data management plan addresses the collection and creation of data, and how data is captured and generated. Questions on potential ethical implications on further use and re-use of the data, copyright and intellectual property rights (IPR) matters need to be answered. Storing, backing-up, accessing, securing and sharing the data are issues of equal importance that need to be closely examined. Difficult decisions have to be taken concerning the responsibility of managing the data, what documents, resources and metadata will be used, and what potential limitations need to be addressed. Preservation and maintenance should not be considered as less important when writing a successful data management plan (University of Sheffield, 2018).

- *Data management*: Data management is the handling of information so that it is stored, preserved and made accessible. Data management practices can be spotted in any project; the better the data is handled the better the result of the project will be (University of Houston, 2018).
- *Digital archives*: In order for print archives to be preserved, optical character recognition machines read characters while scanning the document. The advantage was not only for preservation purposes, but also for users to have access to the archives remotely. A digital archive can also be information in electronic format, which has been preserved for its value (Reitz, 2004, 216).
- *Research data management*: Research data management is a process in which the ultimate goal is to manage research data properly. In addition, it offers the possibility of forging strong relationships and completing projects in a successful manner (TUE, 2018).

Data-intensive science or the 'fourth paradigm' of scientific enquiry (Hey, Tansley and Tolle, 2009) has been a fast growing area that brought together representatives from all academic disciplines to manage, interpret and preserve undiscoverable and untamed data originating from and by any research undertaken globally. As an aftermath, documented practices had to be developed to better define and describe data management procedures in data management planning, data mining, sharing and re-use as well as preserving this data.

Librarians were considered most suitable to undertake data management roles, as they have been successfully structuring and providing access to information and preserving cultural heritage with well-established skill, which they developed over the centuries. Additionally, it has been important to collaborate with the researchers who primarily produce data and thus determine the use of data after it is deposited in a repository or database, and to involve computer scientists who back up and preserve data in perpetuity. Since the role of data stewards (professionals who are responsible for the institutional data governance processes) has been formally established, many people are involved in facilitating research data management processes.

Research funders from all over Europe, Australia and the USA quickly set mandates for any data generated through national funded research to be made publicly available so that it can be stored on open access. Data should be maintained for re-use in a format and cyber-infrastructure that supports long-term (and sometimes heterogeneous) data preservation.

In response, managers of multiple organisations and institutions had to develop data management policies to set out their requirements and procedures which need to be followed for data generated by their employees. Policies are created setting out the general scope and expectations of sharing and re-using research outputs, focusing on researchers' concerns about IPR issues and sensitive data handling, two of the main barriers in choosing the 'open research' path.

Each of the stakeholders plays a unique role in the data management domain and all together they form a powerful alliance for successful data management and preservation. Research data life-cycle models, such as those fostered by the Digital Curation Centre (DCC), UK Data Archive (UKDA), U.S. Geological Survey (USGS) and National Science Foundation (NSF), among others, were developed to illustrate the steps and workflows that datasets follow during their lifespan, and demonstrating the duties and responsibilities that librarians, research-ers and technologists undertake. For a review of some life-cycle models see Ball (2012) and CEOS (2012).

A trigger for developing and implementing data management policies in the higher education sector was funders' mandates in submitting data management plans and research proposals. Practices from organisations and research centres that had been performing data management for years in fields like physics (CERN; Conseil Européen pour la Recherche Nucléaire), space (NASA; National Aeronautics and Space Administration) and environment (NSIDC; National Snow and Ice Data Center) were adapted to get the procedure started. Tools to support data management plans were developed, containing tem-plates that correspond to different funders' requirements for the researcher to choose from and create the plan as required. The latest addition to these tools is software management plans, covering the subsequent use of any software or code used by or developed for the needs of the given research.

Challenges and opportunities

Librarians, information professionals and technologists face some challenges that need to be addressed through advocacy and practical policies:

- *Conservative perceptions* are still holding scientists and faculty away from adapting to open access requirements. The traditional views on sharing information or data have to be dealt with together with concerns about consent and anonymisation as well as data distribution and re-use by others. Researchers' controversial perceptions about the credibility and impact of their research when derived from re-usable data should also be combated.
- *Technical, data model and/or semantic heterogeneity* may create difficulties for both depositors of research data and future users of these data; for example, inconsistency of data formats across collections and various ways of interpreting and storing the same data need to be resolved. Large scale data has become more common and requires adequate data storage and analysis in the long term. Lastly, new types of database infrastructures should be tested that organise data better and make it easily tracked and retrieved.
- *Data management policies* vary from existing institutional policies to those that incorporate a mixture of funders' requirements with detailed guidance on research procedure and provision of support on campus. In addition to data management policies and to facilitate the research data management process within the overall management of an institution, research institutions also develop methodologies and tools, some of which include data audit policies and costings. We provide some examples of data management policies in Table 7.1, of data audit case studies in Table 7.2 and of data management costing tools in Table 7.3. These specialised tools illustrate the complexity of research data management.

Table 7.1 *Examples of data management policies*

Country	Organisation	Description	URL
USA	New York University	"This administrative data management policy sets out how the University of New York manages its data." (New York University, n.d.)	www.nyu.edu/about/policies-guidelines-compliance/policies-and-guidelines/administrative-data-management-policy.html

Table 7.1 *Continued*

Country	Organisation	Description	URL
UK	The University of Edinburgh	"This policy shows step by step how the University of Edinburgh manage its research data." (University of Edinburgh, 2018)	www.ed.ac.uk/information-services/about/policies-and-regulations/research-data-policy
Ireland	University College Cork	"The main goal of this data management policy is to secure any data associated with University College Cork." (University College Cork, 2013)	www.ucc.ie/en/media/support/itpolicies/policies/DataManagementPolicy.pdf
UK	University of Leeds	"This data management policy sets out how data in the University of Leeds will be used." (University of Leeds, 2018)	https://library.leeds.ac.uk/info/14062/research_data_management/68/university_research_data_policy
UK	University of York	"This data management policy sets out how the University of York handles its data." (University of York, n.d.)	www.york.ac.uk/about/departments/support-and-admin/information-services/information-policy/index/research-data-management-policy/#tab-1

Table 7.2 *Examples of institutions which undertook data audit case studies*

Country	Organisation	Description	URL
USA	TVD Associates	This case study explains several points associated with data auditing: why quality data is important, what is a data audit, what steps are involved, and what are the benefits of a data audit (TVD Associates, n.d.)	http://tvdassociates.com/wp-content//uploads/2015/10/TVDA_CaseStudy_MASAE_Data.pdf
UK	University of Oxford	'The project aimed to scope the requirements for digital repository services to manage and curate research data generated by Oxford researchers' (Martinez-Uribe, 2009, 1–9)	www.disc-uk.org/docs/DAF-Oxford.pdf

Table 7.3 *Examples of institutions working on data management costing tools*

Country	Organisation	URL
UK	UK Data Archive	www.data-archive.ac.uk/media/247429/costingtool.pdf
UK	University of St Andrews	www.st-andrews.ac.uk/media/research-data-management/documents/generic/How-to%20Guide%20-%20Costing%20RDM.pdf

Data audit practices

In the past years several data audits have been undertaken in higher education institutions. The Data Audit Framework is an example of a UK, JISC-funded project, which implemented seven such audits at institutions in the UK. Those audits addressed issues around the description, provenance, ownership, location, retention and management of research assets. However, not much has been recorded of a similar type of data audit carried out in a commercial environment, dealing with a vast amount of born digital data such as that generated by an online newspaper. Here is a case study of a mini data audit at the Times of Malta (please see Acknowledgements).

Data management at a commercial environment: a case study of conducting a mini data audit on the data produced by the Times of Malta

This case study explains how librarians and teams in a commercial environment collaborate or interact to provide a traditional newspaper with the best and most current practices on data management so that it can efficiently transition to a modern newspaper by keeping its values and content integrity unalterable by the public.

Introduction

Disruptive innovation (also known as disruptive technology) has been in the forefront for years, creating new needs for customers and pushing stakeholders to follow the digital transformation path. In the world of publishing, electronic versions of traditional printed journals, magazines, books and encyclopaedias emerged to meet online users' needs (most publishers abandoned traditional publishing and focused exclusively on online communities) and nowadays there are even more born digital sources of information. Facebook is one of the disruptive innovations that changed the way people communicate and in the past few years has also evolved as a news resource. Therefore traditional newspapers had to re-assess their business models and integrate their services into the modern environment by launching websites that host their electronic and online material and creating social media accounts where they can share their online content.

For the past three years, the Times of Malta, part of Allied Newspapers, has taken major steps in that direction by following the four stages of disruption. Today it has a website running on a cloud server and is actively involved with the social media platforms of Facebook and Twitter.

This article explores the data management practices that the Times of Malta follows for online content and multimedia, and suggests recommendations for potential improvements. The main objectives were twofold: to understand the overall workflow related to digital content creation, use and management within the organisation, and to synthesise the life cycle of digital objects within the Times of Malta environment.

Methodology

The methodology consisted of holding interviews, desk research and making on-site observations. Representatives of the 170-strong workforce were interviewed, following a protocol which was developed after initial consultations with Chief Technology Officer Donald Tabone, and the data audit framework was adopted after making adjustments to meet the particular needs of a newspaper environment. The interviews gathered the required information in order to better understand how the organisation functions and how employees perform and behave.

Major findings and discussion

These were the three major domains of interest:

- the overall place of the digital object workflows within the organisational culture
- the digital objects' life cycle
- the use of analytics.

Digital object workflows within the organisational culture

The Times of Malta uses an in-house built content management system (CMS) combined with a suite of other tools. Staff members have a good overall knowledge of the capabilities of the system.

Several areas for potential improvement were identified, though the purpose of digital content management units in the organisation chart could not be explored as there was miscommunication with the head of human resources.

The views on some aspects of data management across the company differ (two identified domains are the use of social media and analytics). A further in-depth study would help to identify areas where additional internal training could result in staff achieving a shared vision.

The life cycle of digital objects

The life cycle of digital objects in the Times of Malta office is supported technically by the tools developed by the IT department. There are multiple internal and external users; internal users are those within the Times of Malta who receive adequate support. External users access digital objects which are created by the organisational users according to rights associated with digital objects. Their actions are captured by a range of analytics tools; however observations on use are not added to the original digital objects, but are used and stored as a separate data set. Two versions of the life cycle of digital objects were created following the UK Data Archive's research data lifecycle to identify some differences in the tasks between video or images and online text objects (UK Data Archive, 2016). The two phases preserve and publish are implemented in different sequences in both lifecycles, as presented in figures 7.1 and 7.2.

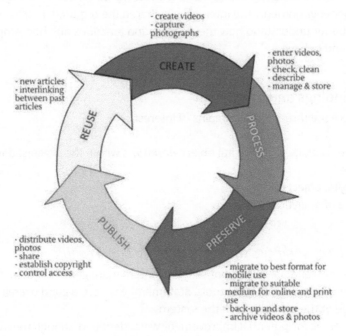

Figure 7.1 *The life cycle of image and video objects*

Areas that could potentially be improved are discussed below.

Creating and editing copy

Lack of detail about the different versions of articles: changes that journalists, editors, sub-editors make to copy are not easily identified and retrievable within

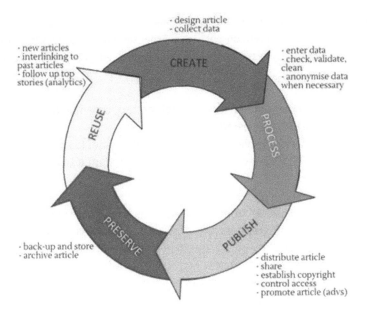

Figure 7.2 *The life cycle of text objects*

editorial teams. A feature similar to cloud drives was suggested so that all members of the team could see and modify the same content and check for past versions that may be of use if copy is required to be reverted.

Persistent identifiers

Lack of persistent identifiers for the digital objects: a unique identification number is given to every online article and forms part of its uniform resource identifier (URI). Unfortunately, despite the beneficial use of this type of identifier, it does not guarantee that the digital object will remain under this URI when a change of servers occurs. A digital object identifier (DOI) was proposed as part of a persistent identifier solution suitable for journal articles (Wikipedia, 2016a).

Rights management and referencing

Intellectual property rights: an omission was identified within the paragraphs on IPR. According to the Times of Malta website,

The text, graphics, images, video, and other data, design, organisation, compilation, look and feel, advertising and all other related protected intellectual property, available through the subscription are our property or the property of our advertisers and/or

Further strengthening and enhancement of the text, targeting the non-subscribed users, was suggested.

It was proposed that a policy on premium content should be developed and refined, and staff should decide how long certain content was offered as premium only.

There are byline references to Reuters and the Press Association when content has been extracted from their platforms. Credits are given to the Times of Malta authors, photographers and videographers as well as to external sources of content and material acquisition. However, online editors lacked discipline in following these procedures. There are a few articles where an image, even text, can be found published without reference to the source.

Preservation

Preservation plan according to the cloud server provider (agreement): the Times of Malta service support agreement requires all content and digital materials to be kept on a cloud server forever and nothing to be deleted. Even though virtual servers, managed databases, storage containers and load balancers provided by the cloud servers are managed by the newspaper's technical staff daily, risk resides in the potential failure of the provider to respond to malicious attacks. This was considered an area for potential improvement.

The same concerns apply to the back-up policy. Higher levels of data security are provided for the use of dedicated servers than with less cost-demanding cloud subscriptions and rentals. Recognising the complexity in having a secondary back-up node, a review of the subject and practices being followed was suggested.

Readers' comments and social media policies

Facebook and Twitter comments: staff responsible for Times of Malta social media appeared to have no priorities and a misunderstanding of their individual duties. There is a controversy among the online editors about their task of moderating comments: one mentions they 'moderate [comment] only those on the website', the other one states that they also moderate a few comments on Facebook. Different persons mentioned Twitter, something that had not been previously mentioned. It was concluded that the editorial team is also responsible for uploading content on social media platforms, lacks organisation and has an inadequate division of duties.

Use of analytics

Analytics have entered the staff's daily routine yet their use is still not captured in a commonly understood and implemented workflow. A Google analytics report is distributed every morning via e-mail, though the people involved with the print issues of the newspaper are not on this emailing list. Further analytics data are obtained from Socionomix, DISQUS, Mandrill and MailChimp, Minely and Alexa, but their data is mostly used by the management.

As most of the online content has been extracted from the print issues, metrics concern both print and online divisions. An additional weakness identified is that those who receive this report do not necessarily pay attention to it (so there is a lack of understanding on the particular ways to use analytics). There is a mixture of feeling about whether these metrics are of use for the staff's daily duties or not. The print editors interpret the traffic of significant online stories as a head start for their stories to be written the next day. For instance, when a local accident occurs the online editors know about it first and then they have an idea about what to publish in the print edition the next day. There is no extensive analysis of why users read particular top stories, such as why some subjects are more popular than others, whether the writing affects readership numbers, and so on. Also, it was noticed that analytics data are not distributed to those editors who work with images and videos, but mostly to managers and editors of text articles.

Recommendations

Here are recommendations for improving the digital object workflows within the organisational culture (Figure 7.3), the digital objects' life cycle (Figure 7.4), and the use of analytics (Figure 7.5 on page 153) at the Times of Malta. They are colour-coded according to their urgency.

These are some additional recommendations:

- establish a preservation plan that guarantees that a back-up of content is always available in a digital space, which is under the full control of the Times of Malta; for initial guidance consult PLATO (n.d.);

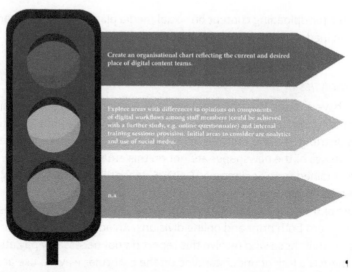

Figure 7.3 *Recommendations for improving digital object workflows within the organisational culture at the Times of Malta*

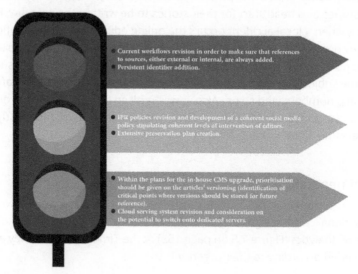

Figure 7.4 *Recommendations for improving digital objects' life cycle at the Times of Malta*

- establish persistent identifiers for data: a good and credible example of persistent identifiers that has existed for years in libraries is that of DOIs (DOI, n.d.), which could be considered and adopted for Times of Malta content;
- online editors and staff should discuss their social media duties.

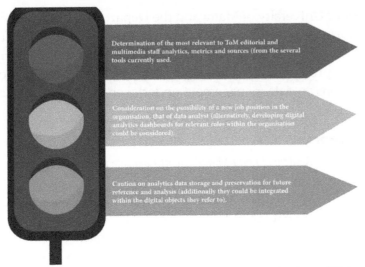

Determination of the most relevant to ToM editorial and multimedia staff analytics, metrics and sources (from the several tools currently used.

Consideration on the possibility of a new job position in the organisation, that of data analyst (alternatively, developing digital analytics dashboards for relevant roles within the organisation could be considered).

Caution on analytics data storage and preservation for future reference and analysis (additionally they could be integrated within the digital objects they refer to).

Figure 7.5 *Recommendations for improving the use of analytics at the Times of Malta*

Summary

Data-intensive science is accelerating developments in library science and computer science, and librarians and computer scientists are more confident than before in responding to technological issues and researchers' queries and requests in the collaborative environment that they have created.

Researchers' knowledge and familiarisation with the data management planning stage of data lifecycles is increasing, data stewardship programmes assist this pursuit, and tools that support researchers' needs make it easier for them to perform data management activities.

Finally, data management practices correspond to environments beyond research. We hope that this chapter will inspire librarians, bring together more stakeholders and create collaborations within a spectrum of environments, with the aspiration of creating better managed and preserved data distribution systems.

Acknowledgements

The case study at the Times of Malta was facilitated with the collaboration of the Department of Library Information and Archive

Sciences of University of Malta and the Department of Library Science and Information Systems of ATEI of Thessaloniki under the funding of COST action KnowEscape, chaired by Dr Andrea Scharnhorst. Findings presented in this chapter are part of ongoing work for dissertations on data management undertaken at ATEI of Thessaloniki.

Bibliography

Ball, A. (2012) *Review of Data Management Lifecycle Models,* University of Bath, http://opus.bath.ac.uk/28587/.

CEOS (2012) *Data Life Cycle Models and Concepts, CEOS Version 1.2.* CEOS.WGISS.DSIG.TN01 Issue 1.2 April 2012, 90 pp, http://ceos.org/ourwork/workinggroups/wgiss/documents/.

Data Asset Framework (n.d.) Data Asset Framework: four steps to effective data management, www.data-audit.eu/.

Data Seal of Approval (2015) The Guidelines 2014–2015, https://www.datasealofapproval.org/media/filer_public/2013/09/27/guidelines_2014-2015.pdf.

DOI (n.d.) Digital Object Identifier, www.doi.org/factsheets/Identifier_Interoper.html.

Funder Data-Related Mandates (2016) Johns Hopkins University Data Management Services, http://dms.data.jhu.edu/data-management-resources/plan-research/funders-data-sharing-requirement/funder-data-related-mandates-and-public-access-plans/.

HATII (2009) *Data Audit Framework Methodology,* version 1.8, Humanities Advanced Technology and Information Institute, University of Glasgow, www.data-audit.eu/DAF_Methodology.pdf.

Hey, T., Tansley, S. and Tolle, K. (eds) (2009) *The Fourth Paradigm: data-intensive scientific discovery,* Microsoft Research.

Martinez-Uribe, L. (2009) Using the Data Audit Framework: an Oxford case study, University of Oxford, www.disc-uk.org/docs/DAF-Oxford.pdf.

NDA (n.d.) National Institute of Mental Health Data Archive (NDA), https://data-archive.nimh.nih.gov/.

New York University (n.d.) Administrative Data Management Policy, www.nyu.edu/about/policies-guidelines-compliance/policies-and-guidelines/administrative-data-management-policy.html.

PLATO. (n.d.) Decision making tool for digital preservation, www.ifs.tuwien.ac.at/dp/plato/intro/.

Reitz, J. (2004) Digital Archives, in *Dictionary for Library and Information Science*, Libraries Unlimited, https://books.google.co.uk/books?redir_esc=y&id=f9WH9soOBrUC&q= digital+archives+#v=onepage&q&f=false.

Techopedia.com (2018) What Is a Data Audit?, www.techopedia.com/definition/28032/data-audit.

TUE (2018) What is Research Data Management?, Technische Universiteit Eindhoven, www.tue.nl/en/university/library/education-research-support/scientific-publishing/data-coach/general-terms-and-background/what-is-research-data-management/.

TVD Associates (n.d.) *Data Auditing: a proven process for success*, TVD Associates, http://tvdassociates.com/wp-content//uploads/2015/10/TVDA_CaseStudy_MASAE_Data.pdf.

UK Data Archive (2016) Create and Manage Data: research data lifecycle, www.data-archive.ac.uk/create-manage/life-cycle.

UK Data Archive (2018) About the Archive, www.data-archive.ac.uk/about/archive.

University College Cork (2013) Data Management Policy, University College Cork, www.ucc.ie/en/media/support/itpolicies/policies/DataManagementPolicy.pdf.

University of Edinburgh (2018) Research Data Management Policy, www.ed.ac.uk/information-services/about/policies-and-regulations/research-data-policy.

University of Houston (2018) Data Management and Sharing, www.uh.edu/research/compliance/data-mgmt-plan/.

University of Leeds (2018) Research Data Management Policy, https://library.leeds.ac.uk/info/14062/research_data_management/68/university_research_data_policy.

University of Sheffield (2018) Data Management Planning, University Library, University of Sheffield, www.sheffield.ac.uk/library/rdm/dmp.

University of York (n.d.) Research Data Management Policy, www.york.ac.uk/about/departments/support-and-admin/information-services/information-policy/index/research-data-management-policy/#tab-1.

Wikipedia (2016a) Digital Object Identifier, https://en.wikipedia.org/wiki/Digital_object_identifier.

8

Access restrictions

Gillian Oliver

Introduction

Traditionally, archives have been characterised by restrictions on access for two main reasons: because of the nature of the type of information represented by archival records, and the need to protect unique artefacts. However, all the settings have changed in today's digital environment, which necessitates questioning and re-evaluating our approaches to access. Networked technologies have substantially lowered barriers and put archives in the global information landscape. This process is not always straightforward – the complexity of digitisation arrangements, and in particular agreements for joint digitisation initiatives of archives with external partners, contribute to make artefacts available in digital form, but might be bound with access restrictions as highlighted by Trudy Huskamp Peterson in Chapter 2. While these are interesting phenomena, the aim of our chapter is to highlight the perspectives on access restrictions that reflect the nature of the archival materials and their use.

This chapter begins by exploring traditional views of access provision, and then reflects on the disjuncture between highly publicised freedom of information initiatives such as WikiLeaks and current professional practice. By way of contrast, the need to recognise cultural imperatives to restrict access is discussed, using the example of New Zealand Māori perspectives. This example also illustrates the dimension of access which contributes to 'giving a voice' to minorities and in some cases puts access in the centre of human rights movements. The chapter concludes by calling for a much more nuanced and culturally appropriate view of access rights and restrictions.

Access – of lesser importance to archivists?

It can be argued that access considerations may be accorded the lowest priority by archivists, as is illustrated by this summary of the skills needed by an archivist taken from the Australian Society of Archivists' website. Archivists need to know:

- what records and archives are, and how they have evolved in modern society
- how to collect archives and how to assess the long-term value of records
- how to look after archives
- how to understand legal issues and responsibilities including copyright, confidentiality, privacy and access
- how to arrange and describe archives for management control and to make them available
- how to provide services for those wishing to make use of the archives (Australian Society of Archivists, 2013).

Access is not mentioned until the fourth bullet point, and then in conjunction with restrictions on access. It is only the final point that refers to users. By way of contrast, the goals of librarians as reflected in the core values of their Australian professional association are significantly different, with 'access' signalled as the leading value:

- promotion of the free flow of information and ideas through open access to recorded knowledge, information, and creative works
- connection of people to ideas
- commitment to literacy, information literacy and learning
- respect for the diversity and individuality of all people
- preservation of the human record
- excellence in professional service to our communities
- partnerships to advance these values (ALIA, 2010).

Understanding why this different prioritisation has been accorded to access by these two occupations helps provide insight into the impact of access drivers on digital initiatives in the two domains. The motivator for these differences lies in the fundamentally diverse purposes that characterise the work of archivists and the work of librarians. Monash University's Information Continuum Model (first described in an addendum to Upward, 2000) articulates this very clearly, distinguishing the primary purpose of record keepers (archivists and records managers) as managing information as evidence, for the purpose of accountability. In contrast, the primary focus of librarians is to manage information as knowledge, for awareness. This focus on information as evidence necessitates much more care and attention having to be paid to considering who should be able to access the archives, and when that access can be permitted – today, or at some given point in the future. If archivists are not regarded as trustworthy custodians, then there is a risk of records not being entrusted to them. This point leads to another important reason why access has not traditionally been highly prioritised.

The prioritisation of evidential values in relation to archives means that the context in which they have been created and maintained (for example, a workplace or home environment) is as important as their informational content. Therefore archives, unlike library-type materials, are unique. As Laura Millar points out, even if there are a dozen copies of minutes made for distribution to assorted committee members, the uniqueness of the minutes lies in their relationship to other records maintained by each individual (Millar, 2010, 9).

Because of this uniqueness extra attention has to be paid to protection and preservation. Archives are irreplaceable, so in the paper world access to users is provided only within a controlled environment – generally a carefully monitored reading room. It is not surprising therefore that access has traditionally been accorded the lowest priority of an archivist's responsibilities. Primary concerns focus on appraising (selecting), protecting and preserving.

In conjunction with this duty to protect and preserve is the imperative for archivists to balance access requirements against the need to protect in accordance with social and organisational imperatives. These social and organisational imperatives vary according to the particular sector and environment, but include legal, organisational, donor and cultural considerations.

Legal considerations

In the public sector, archival legislation may specify a period of time for which records have to remain closed. For instance, the Australian Archives Act imposes a blanket restriction on public access for non-exempt Commonwealth records for a number of decades (National Archives of Australia, 2013). The period of time has been progressively reduced from 50 years; for current transfers the norm is 20 years. In contrast, freedom of information legislation mandates public access to current government information, unless other specified considerations (for example, national security) come into play. Another primary influence on access restrictions is privacy legislation, which addresses the need to protect personal information about individuals. The impact of privacy requirements extends far beyond current information-handling concerns and in some cases permanent restriction is imposed. For instance, adoption case files at Archives New Zealand have the following note relating to access, which covers not only the records themselves, but also the lists of those files: 'All adoption files contain information of a highly private and confidential nature and, under the current provisions of the Adoption Act 1955 and Adult Adoption Act 1985, are permanently restricted. Records lists are also permanently restricted' (Archives New Zealand, 2010).

For further information on legal considerations, and particularly of copyright implications, see Chapter 3 by Guy Pessach and Chapter 4 by Oleksandr Pastukhov in this edited collection. There are also examples of privacy aspects in medical records management, which have implications for academic research where this data would help to develop new treatments; for an overview see Marinič (2015).

Organisational and donor considerations

In conjunction with, or in the absence of, legislatively mandated requirements, a closure period may be negotiated with an agency or individual transferring or donating records to an archival repository. The archives institution must be able to provide an assurance that public access will only be permitted under certain conditions. Usually this is a time period consisting of decades or more into the future. For example, the records of New Zealand politician Leslie Gandar had the following restriction noted when this chapter was written in 2013:

'Access to any material less than 25 years old will require the permission of the Chief Librarian. Access to Cabinet papers less than 25 years old requires the permission of the Secretary of the Cabinet Office.' Currently the records of Leslie Gandar are displayed as having no access restrictions in the National Library of New Zealand (Gandar, n.d.).

Reasons for restricted access can range from commercial sensitivity (not wanting to reveal any secrets of success to competitors) to personal sensitivity (avoiding causing distress or embarrassment to living persons or their family members). It can easily be seen that a consequence of archives refusing to apply and administer restrictions could result in records not being transferred or donated. If there is no legislative mandate to transfer records with archival value to a designated repository, goodwill has to be maintained at all costs.

Challenges to traditional access views

The advent of WikiLeaks (http://wikileaks.org/About.html) has however profoundly challenged the professional perspectives of Western archivists to access. Massive quantities of the types of documents that would under normal circumstances be transferred to a government archival authority and only made available to the public some very distant time in the future could suddenly be read by anyone anywhere, so long as they had an internet connection. In the case of WikiLeaks the documents were cables containing confidential communications between US embassies worldwide and the State Department in Washington DC. This startling availability was immediately condemned by the US government and its allies as endangering the lives of individuals working in the security services. However, no shocking incidents have been reported, and the content of the cables has provided considerable insight into the behind the scenes activities that are part and parcel of the diplomatic mission, with often frank assessments of people in high profile roles.

What is more, the WikiLeaks cables have been simply made available, without the application of any archival methodologies. In the absence of a professional archival framework it is relatively straightforward to foresee difficulties in the future; in the long term being able to access and interpret the cables is likely to be extremely problematic. Nevertheless, this case has effectively turned the archival endeavour on its head and demonstrated that access could indeed be prioritised. It has also raised serious questions about the archivist's readiness to restrict, and what this means about our role in promoting established power hierarchies.

Cultural considerations

The discussion of access restrictions so far has been very firmly centred on the paradigms and worldviews of the developed world. There are also cultural imperatives which require that archives should only be accessible by members of a particular societal unit. These may (rarely) be embodied in legislation, but may also lead to organisational or donor negotiations, as mentioned above. However, they are significant enough to be singled out for discussion, as in many cases the need to apply restrictions may even result in separate repositories being established. This is particularly true for indigenous cultures, and New Zealand Māori perspectives provide a view into this often unacknowledged and unrecognised domain.

The Māori worldview of knowledge is known as mātauranga Māori. Whatarangi Winiata has provided a fascinating 'translation' of traditional archival concepts into this Māori world view, including access; restrictions on access are a key consideration. Winiata explains that access will be made available to selected items, and emphasises that non-documentary records such as artworks can also be 'read'. However, access must not be considered as a given, or as a right. Written records 'can be read if the holders agree' and furthermore:

> Repositories of mātauranga Māori will follow what can be described as their five-way test in coming to a decision on whether to give an enquirer access to mātauranga Māori held by the repository. The repository will want to know whether the person wanting access has the ability to:
>
> 1 Receive the information with the utmost accuracy;
> 2 Store the information with integrity beyond doubt;
> 3 Apply appropriate judgement in the use of the information; and
> 4 Pass on the information appropriately.
>
> (Winiata, 2005, 16)

These concerns to restrict access, and to guard against unauthorised or inappropriate access, especially for archives of human right cases, war crime archives and other records which can touch on personal violations, are just as important in the digital environment, and more problematic to administer if attempts are made to use 'off-the-shelf' repository software. Honiana Love and Clare Hall provide a vivid account of the development of a digital archive to support the revitalisation of a regional language, Taranaki reo. The archive contains local digital materials, and one of the motivators for its establishment was to allow for the digital 'repatriation' of historic documents in Taranaki reo, held by national archival institutions. A major problem that Love and Hall encountered related to access. The digital archive was developed using Kete (www.kete.net.nz/), an open source software product developed by the New Zealand library community:

> What we didn't consider was how different our world view might be from that of library communities. . . . The first trap we fell into was imagining our Kete could be 'tweaked' to meet our needs, when in fact we needed to consider a Māori world view from the get-go. This meant secure areas where knowledge might only be available to a few – worlds away from the library vision of information available to all who care to look.
>
> (Love and Hall, 2011–12, 28)

The need to balance access with authenticity and security considerations meant that what appeared to be a very feasible software platform for the archive would only be appropriate if significant customisation occurred, which required sophisticated technical expertise.

Conclusion

The digital environment, disintermediation of information and the ability of citizens to acquire covertly and then provide access to vast quantities of supposedly confidential records is a significant watershed, which is testing archivists' attitudes to access. Restricting access to archives has traditionally been the default position, not least because of the need to protect and preserve fragile, unique sources of information. Debate generally centres on rights and responsibilities with respect to official information and the extent to which the rhetoric of open government is being met. However, it is important to take a much more nuanced view of access issues, and not to be sidetracked into a one-eyed view of freedom of information at all costs. Different cultural mores and attitudes must be taken into account, and alternative perspectives of knowledge paradigms represented in our decision making. In considering the archival mission in the digital environment Frank Upward, Sue McKemmish and Barbara Reed identified a number of key ideas that need to be explored. These include using online technologies as an opportunity to develop collaborative archival spaces, which can be shared by communities but allow configuration for differentiated access, and also to use WikiLeaks type cases as opportunities to re-examine professional practice (Upward, McKemmish and Reed, 2011, 236).

Practitioners who have to implement sensitivity reviews and make decisions on access rights can in some cases follow institutional guidelines. An excellent recent example is the publication of The National Archives of the UK, *Access to Public Records: a toolkit for practitioners involved in the sensitivity review and transfer of public records to The National Archives and other archives services* (2015).

In conclusion, restrictions on access are and will continue to be a necessary component to be taken into consideration when developing digital archives. But there are many ambiguities surrounding just when, how and for whom restrictions are imposed. This is a key challenge facing archivists today. The way forward does not consist of simply discarding the older, more traditional restrictions, but it is necessary to renegotiate access provisions to ensure that they are appropriate for all communities.

References

ALIA (2010) ALIA Vision, Mission, Objects, Australian Library and Information Association.

Archives New Zealand (2010) Adoption – client files (7244), series access statement, http://archway.archives.govt.nz/ViewEntity.do?code=7244.

Australian Society of Archivists (2013) About the Archival Profession, https://www.archivists.org.au/learning-publications/the-archival-profession/.

Gandar, L. W. (n.d.) Alexander Turnbull Library, Gandar, Leslie Walter, 1919–1994 papers, https://natlib.govt.nz/records/23189985?search%5Bil%5D%5Bcollection%5D=Manuscripts+Collection&search%5Bpath%5D=items&search%5Btext%5D=gandar.

Love, H. and Hall, C. (2011–12) Ka Puta, Ka Ora: digital archiving and the revitalisation of Taranaki reo, *Archifacts*, October 2011–April 2012, 25–34.

Marinič, M. (2015) Privacy in Archive Health Records, *Health Science Journal*, **9** (3), 1–6.

Millar, L. (2010) *Archives: principles and practices*, Facet Publishing.

National Archives of Australia (2013) Legislation that Affects How Your Agency Manages its Records, www.naa.gov.au/records-management/strategic-information/standards/recordslegislation.aspx.

The National Archives (2015) *Access to Public Records: a toolkit for practitioners involved in the sensitivity review and transfer of public records to The National Archives and other archives services*, www.nationalarchives.gov.uk/documents/information-management/access-to-public-records.pdf.

Upward, F. (2000) Modelling the Continuum as Paradigm Shift in Recordkeeping and Archiving Process, and Beyond – a personal reflection, *Records Management Journal*, **10** (3), 115–39.

Upward, F., McKemmish, S. and Reed, B. (2011) Archivists and Changing Social and Information Spaces: a continuum approach to recordkeeping and archiving in online cultures, *Archivaria*, **72**, 197–237.

Winiata, W. (2005) Survival of Māori as a People and Māori Archives, *Archifacts*, April, 9–19.

9

Citizen science: two case studies in oral history research

Milena Dobreva and Edel Jennings

Introduction

There have been many participatory approaches to digital cultural heritage in recent years, with a groundbreaking work on archives by Sexton and Flinn (2013). There is particularly prominent interest in the applications of crowd sourcing (Ridge, 2014) and citizen science in this domain (Dobreva, 2016). One area where participatory approaches could be particularly beneficial is oral history research; the advantage of appealing to the wisdom of the crowd is to attract greater numbers of contributors to the collection of histories on a particular topic. Involving a wider network of informants should ideally allow more content collecting and refining of information through the memories of participants.

Oral history projects can follow different designs and one recent trend is to involve interviewers as voluntary contributors after providing sufficient context on the research and interview process. Volunteers can also help in transcribing and curating interviews. In some cases, people from the same community or even family may be involved since they have the advantage of knowing the interviewee, which can be beneficial for topics where there are no areas of sensitivity. In other cases, spreading the word in the community can help to identify potential contributors to the project.

This chapter explores two case studies on oral history projects implemented in two countries (Ireland and Malta) and on different topics (rural place names and tattoo art history). In Ireland, six teenagers aged 15 or 16, from two schools, applied to take part in the project within three weeks in November 2014. In Malta, university students were involved in the various stages of the project, from holding and transcribing interviews to populating digital content on an institutional repository.

Looking at two case studies helps us to better understand the dynamic of early involvement of volunteers and to explore the potential benefits for projects that require a high level of dedication.

Participatory approaches in archives

Staff in memory institutions are interested in involving members of the general public in contributing to the creation and/or refinement of digital content. One of the popular ways of engaging citizens is crowd sourcing; in 2011 Johan Oomen and Lora Aroyo proposed a typology, which looks at several ways of engaging citizens: through correction and transcription, contextualisation, complementing collections, classification, co-curation and crowdfunding (Oomen and Aroyo, 2011). Another participatory approach is citizen science (for multiple examples see Liew et al., 2015; Ridge, 2014), where citizens contribute to specific research questions but frequently the technique to achieve this is crowd sourcing.

Projects involving citizen science in archives can be implemented by individual amateur researchers, for example creating databases supporting the study of passport applications at the collection of the National Archives of Malta (see Caruana, 2016). But in many cases this is a collective activity and depends on the contribution of multiple volunteers.

Table 9.1 summarises the use of citizen science within memory institutions.

Table 9.1 *Citizen science and memory institutions*

Question	Explanation
Why?	Citizen science aims to support research This method benefits community engagement and can help when institutions initiating it are under-resourced
Who?	Co-ordinated by researchers and heritage professionals; involves volunteers
What?	Volunteers can contribute to a range of well-defined tasks
How?	Nowadays with the use of technological platforms, most often mobile devices
When?	Volunteers can contribute in their free time (using the so-called cognitive surplus)

To contribute to better understanding of the practical implementation of citizen science in the cultural heritage domain, we will look into two recent examples. The main focus of our interest is methodological – identifying elements which work well; we are also particularly interested in the point of engagement of volunteers and argue that early engagement during the project set-up is beneficial to better understand the potential contributions and sustain interest.

Case study: place names in rural Ireland

An oral history pilot on rural place names in Ireland had been implemented within the European Commission-funded Civic Epistemologies Project in 2014 and 2015 (Jennings, 2015). This pilot aimed to explore the impact of the contribution of teenagers in the design of a citizen science project, expanding their involvement beyond the mere data collection. Observations were made of six teenagers aged between 15 and 16, from two schools, who took part in the pilot in 2014 and 2015. The teenagers first participated in a three-week long placement in November 2014, where they met specialists of various profiles, provided feedback on the design of the pilot, and took part in interviewing a group of elderly people and transcribing the interview records.

The intergenerational digital toolkit developed to record heritage in the Civic Epistemologies Project pilot consists of a website co-designed and developed by the students and a suite of free applications for smartphones and laptops. Audio recordings were made using the default voice recorder on a Samsung Galaxy android smart phone. Audacity was used to edit the audio files. SoundCloud was used to store and share the published audio files. WordPress was used to develop the website. Adobe Creative Suite was used to design graphics and handouts. Various WordPress audio, map and social media plugins were integrated to enable users to interact with the project recordings in different ways. The pilot used a website platform showcasing some of the audio recordings made during the participatory meeting as reference examples, along with further recordings made by the students with their relatives (Civic Epistemologies, 2015). It offered distilled, simplified methodologies for recording place names and oral histories, technical tips and a blog documenting students' experience working on the project.

An added value in this citizen-led approach is that the recording and digitisation of cultural heritage created an opportunity for face-to-face intergenerational exchange that might not otherwise have occurred, which potentially has a transformative personal value for the participants beyond the gathering of cultural repositories.

It is essential that citizen powered projects, which rely on people volunteering their time and intellectual efforts, dedicate significant resources to organisational issues and the engagement process. The voluntary ad hoc nature of public engagement with citizen science projects means that planning engagement events often involves unknowns and uncertainties. It is challenging to do this while simultaneously leaving the definition of project tasks sufficiently open to citizens' contributions.

We considered the various perspectives of transition year students, schools, senior citizens and experts in the fields of place names, oral history, community cultural heritage and architectural conservation, in developing a motivational matrix for participation. We wrote a clear engagement proposition and plan outlining the project goals, and the nature of tasks citizens could be expected to undertake. Initially labelled 'Digital Remap', the plan was a key design artefact in our engagement strategy. Various citizen outreach and engagement events were organised to accommodate the volunteers' habits and diverse timetables.

Trust is fundamental in citizen engagement. The role of a local third level educational institution in the project, the Waterford Institute of Technology, offered recognition and credibility to potential contributors. Additionally, this ensured ethical approval was obtained from the Institute's ethics board before approaching participants. Consent forms were drawn up with due consideration of the European responsible research innovation guidelines. Written and verbal consent of all participants was sought and recorded. All participants knew they could opt out at any stage.

Engagement of young adults and senior citizens

We approached local secondary schools in order to find teenagers interested in participating in this pilot study. We obtained the approval of each school's transition year co-ordinator for the project, as a prerequisite to engaging with teenagers under age 18, following stringent ethical guidelines.

Initially, neither school teachers nor the teenagers were familiar with the idea of citizen science for cultural heritage, but they quickly grasped the potential value for school history projects in developing an accessible digital toolkit for ordinary (non-researcher) citizens to preserve local heritage. We offered four non-paid work experience placements for teenagers via the school's transition year programmes as an incentive to participate – inviting students to apply who were interested in careers in cultural heritage, social science, media, research or digital technologies, and had experience or interest in working with older people.

These six teenagers were digital natives who reported that they and their peers were immersed in digital entertainment, online information and communications services. They recorded and facilitated their social lives via a plethora of social networking services. Usage and access to technologies among this group was not uniform, which is significant for future youth citizen science planning. Some had very basic phones, very old home computers and no experience in creating digital artefacts, while others had access to a variety of digital devices and were confident and competent in using unfamiliar technologies. Each of the six students brought a unique viewpoint to the project. They embraced the pilot project, and took ownership of their roles in its implementation, often going beyond the requirements of their work experience placement. In some cases, the students also created audio recordings in their own time with relatives to supplement the projects' recordings, and test the proposed methodologies and guidelines.

Finding senior citizens who were willing to participate in the pilot study was vital to its feasibility. We found that connecting with older people in the community required sensitivity and flexibility, and ideally leveraged pre-existing community relationships to establish trust. Several senior citizens from a local family heritage group in Tramore, County Waterford, agreed to take part, though just two men were available to attend the participatory meeting. This group, which was originally formed through collaboration on local heritage research with a historian, meets weekly in a local community centre. Other senior relatives of the student volunteers also contributed to place-based heritage recordings.

Many older retired people are busy with social lives, hobbies and supporting families, and some are challenged by managing the care of others or have health issues. The information and place-based cultural material collected from senior citizens is often the fabric of their memories and lives – it is personal to them and ought to be treated with the utmost respect. It is important that all citizens are fully informed about all the intended future use of recorded material, and privacy matters related to sharing technologies. In this pilot we proposed that interviewers should own the citizen science project audio files; in most cases they were related to the interviewee. Therefore family relationships and knowledge could guide which information was shared publicly from interviews, and manage the conditions and extent of sharing, and even remove audio segments if preferred at any stage.

Ownership of materials collected in citizen science projects, authorship and copyright would clearly benefit from further clarification.

Case study: REL•INK – Indelible Narratives

REL•INK– Indelible Narratives is a project implemented in co-operation between the Malta Maritime Museum, Heritage Malta and the Library Information and

Archive Sciences Department, University of Malta. REL·INK is supported by the Malta Arts Fund. To match the nature of this community project, the team decided to have as its main website communication channel a Facebook page (Facebook, n.d.).

REL·INK is a community and citizen science based project, which looks at tattooing in elderly Maltese male informants, aged over 80 years of age, who worked on the waterfront either as stevedores, fishermen, longshoremen, dockers, sailors or stewards, or in the Royal Navy, Merchant Navy or related occupations.

Its intention is to document early 20th-century tattoo designs in the Maltese population, with the aim of building a digital archive that will feature as a University of Malta open source resource. Our research also looks at the Mediterranean port city of Marseille as one possible cultural cross-pollination point for tattoo culture in Malta.

Evidence was collected through a combination of research methods. Passport applications from the end of the 19th century and the beginning of the 20th century were checked for mention of tattoos. This established that about 15% of the applicants who had maritime professions had tattoos. In some cases, there were short descriptions of the tattoos but no relevant photographic materials of the tattoo images. The investigation of the passport applications helped to establish that the profession of a tattoo artist had been used on at least one occasion within the collection of passport applications from the National Archives of Malta.

A major challenge in this project was the collection of images. There are no specialised collections of tattoo photographs which can be consulted and images are very difficult to locate. Working with people who have memories of tattooed members of the family is one of the approaches used to expand this research; advertising on social media platforms and using media publicity were two other methods employed to invite contributions from the community.

The project involved the following activities:

- preparation of criteria and a research process with partners
- an outreach community exchange event
- archival research (collecting supporting evidence on tattooing from passport applications and prison records)
- analyses of documentary evidence
- inputting the documentation gathered into the curatorial and artistic process
- preparing an exhibition REL*INK Indelible Narratives in the Malta Maritime Museum (7 October to 30 December 2017, extended for two months into 2018, following the significant interest it aroused); there was much personal engagement with the exhibition: several attendees provided additional information on historical tattoos from their family archives

- a public talk and presentation to showcase tattoo design culture in the elderly population
- preparation of aspects of project-related documentation and resource gathering for eventual hosting on an open access repository of the University of Malta as a designated collection for research purposes.

One particular challenge addressed with this project was the collection of evidence from a variety of sources. There are a whole range of topics for which the evidence is scattered – and the project intends to fill some of the gaps related to questions like:

- Who were the people who acquired tattoos in the early 20th century in Malta? Was it a widespread practice?
- Was it an overwhelmingly male practice?
- Was it confined to specific social groups or professions?
- At what age did they acquire tattoos?
- Was it common in younger people?
- Was it common in older people?
- Was it more prevalent in illiterate people?
- Where were tattoos mostly located on the body?
- What were the themes that were popular as designs? What themes were common?
- What size of tattoos were preferred (in width and length of design)? What composite elements of tattoo were common? What was the use of colour?
- Is there anything inherently specific to the culture?
- Is there any evidence that the practice was mostly related to the maritime profession? Is there any evidence it was mostly associated with criminality?
- Can any generalisations be made?

Besides documentary evidence, the oral history component allowed us to gain insights into the perceptions and practices related to tattooing. The interviews helped to establish a range of relevant details when investigating the following questions:

- Who were the tattoo artists (name, nickname, general or detailed description)?
- Where were they located?
- What was their tattoo parlour like?
- Did they have their own flash designs?
- Did they trace the design?
- Did they do this freehand?
- What instruments did they use?

- Were they using new technology, e.g. a tattooing machine?
- Did they use older 'hand poke' methods?
- How much did a tattoo cost?
- Did tattooists adhere to hygiene rules?
- Did they use any antiseptic?

The example of REL•INK demonstrated that incomplete or sometimes lost records from the near past can to some extent be complemented with memories and materials from personal collections. This is a very interesting and rewarding type of work – but the personal involvement and time investment of project members is very substantial.

Discussion and conclusions

We took two examples of oral history projects that apply citizen science methods in oral history research. We identified the following similarities in these two case studies:

- *Intergenerational involvement*: both case studies illustrate initiatives seeking to involve younger generations in capturing aspects of the life of previous generations.
- *Complexity of involvement*: crowd-sourcing projects in the memory institutions domain in their popular typology are mainly used to support specific activities according to Oomen and Aroyo (2011): correction and transcription, contextualisation, complementing collections, classification, co-curation and crowdfunding. The case studies presented here cannot be attributed to one individual activity but combine collecting new materials (complementing collections) and contextualisation.

These are some of the noticeable differences between the case studies:

- the nature of the data collected (place names in the Irish project versus visual materials or descriptions of such visual materials in the Maltese one)
- the use of citizen science (in REL•INK it is mostly aimed at expanding contributors' base, while in the rural archaeology pilot it was used also to refine the design and use of the data collection).

However, reflecting on the cases jointly was particularly helpful with regard to the nature of intergenerational involvement. It might be strange to state that such projects help to restore and expand dialogue between generations, and they have unexpected but welcome consequences. This is yet another instance of digital engagement, which can contribute to joint activities and sharing between generations.

References

Caruana, M. (2016) Analysis of Data from Maltese Passport Applications Held at the National Archives of Malta: a new digital resource, *New Review of Information Networking*, **21** (1), 52–62.

Civic Epistemologies (2015) Pilot on Archaeology in Rural Ireland, www.civic-epistemologies.eu/outcomes/pilot/pilot-on-archaeology-in-rural-ireland/.

Dobreva, M. (2016) Collective Knowledge and Creativity: the future of citizen science in the humanities, in Kunifuji, S., Papadopoulos, G., Skulimowski, A. and Kacprzyk, J. (eds), *Knowledge, Information and Creativity Support Systems*, Advances in Intelligent Systems and Computing, 565–73.

Facebook (n.d.) REL*INK, www.facebook.com/pg/RelInk-Indelible-Narratives-1581731032130987/about/.

Jennings, E. (2015) *D4.1 Ethnographic Pilot Report*, Civic Epistemologies, www.civic-epistemologies.eu/wp-content/uploads/2014/07/CIVIC-EPISTEMOLOGIES_D4.1_Ethnograhic-Pilot-Report_v1.0.pdf.

Liew, C. L., Wellington, S., Oliver, G. and Perkins, R. (2015) Social Media in Libraries and Archives: applied with caution/Les Medias Sociaux dans les Bibliothèques et les Archives: appliqués avec prudence, *Canadian Journal of Information and Library Science*, **39** (3), 377–96, www.muse.jhu.edu/article/598452.

Oomen, J. and Aroyo, L. (2011) Crowdsourcing in the Cultural Heritage Domain: opportunities and challenges, in *Proceedings of the 5th International Conference on Communities and Technologies*, New York, 138–49.

Ridge, M. (2014) *Crowdsourcing our Cultural Heritage*, Ashgate.

Sexton, A. and Flinn, A. (2013) Research on Community Heritage: moving from collaborative research to participatory and co-designed research practice, Prato, https://studylib.net/doc/12864587/research-on-community-heritage--moving-from-collaborative.

Afterword

Welcome again! Arriving at this point means that you navigated a range of topics and points of view on digital archives. We hope that this collection helped you to understand better this complex domain. As we stated earlier, this is not a manual which would guide you in what to do. The digital world is very diverse and each institution is looking for the right combination of content, services and engagement with its communities. We wanted to provide an opportunity to explore the different aspects of the domain and to give a taste of some of the tools of the trade. If you were a complete novice in this area, we hope this book gave you a sound overview of the various aspects of digital archives. If you are at an intermediary level, we hope it helped you to build your knowledge further. And if you are an expert in a particular domain, we hope that the breadth of the examples and points of view helped to expand the depth of your knowledge.

We are very conscious that a book which brings multiple points of view is a good way to expand readers' understanding. You had a chance to walk in the shoes of archivists, digital humanists, lawyers, information scientists, economists and policy researchers. This wealth of perspectives may feel only a starting point in a longer journey and here we would like to point out some additional publications which could help you explore further.

If you developed a particular interest in engagement with digital archives, you might find useful the edited collection *Engaging with Records and Archives: histories and theories*, edited by Fiorella Foscarini, Heather MacNeil, Bonnie Mak and Gillian Oliver (Facet Publishing, 2016). We were fortunate to have Gillian as one of the contributors to this book (Chapter 8).

You may also check a book which will shortly be available at around the time our book is published: *Community Archives*, Volume 2, Sustaining Memory, edited by Jeannette A. Bastian and Andrew Flinn (Facet Publishing, forthcoming 2018).

If you feel that you would like to further explore the territory of digital humanities and the role of memory institutions, a valuable source for you would be *Developing Digital Scholarship: emerging practices in academic libraries*, edited by Alison Mackenzie and Lindsey Martin (Facet Publishing, 2016). We are not aware of a book which presents this area from the perspective of archivists, but in the context of the current convergence of practices the book can provide good general understanding and give ideas on the knowledge and practical skills that are becoming part of the information professional's profile.

Finally, if you are interested in the legislative aspects of digital archives, you could consult *Open Licensing for Cultural Heritage*, by Gill Hamilton and Fred Saunderson (Facet Publishing, 2017).

The economic and policy aspects are not covered extensively in monographs to the best of our knowledge, but including them to this collection is helping readers to appreciate the multifaceted nature of digital archives and the fabric of relationships with other areas.

We would like to express again our gratitude to the contributors for their dedication and inspiration. This book can be seen as the beginning of a journey – for the publishers to put together further books which would provoke and guide the readers to insights on newly formed trends of work. And for the readers to continue their journey into all ways of transmitting our human culture and knowledge to the digital space.

Index